RE:CRAFTED
INTERPRETATIONS OF CRAFT IN CONTEMPORARY ARCHITECTURE AND INTERIORS
MARC KRISTAL

THE MONACELLI PRESS

Library of Congress Cataloging-in-Publication Data
Kristal, Marc.
Re:crafted : interpretations of craft in contemporary architecture and interiors / Marc Kristal. — 1st ed.
p. cm.
Includes bibliographical references.
ISBN 978-1-58093-276-9
1. Architecture, Modern—21st century. 2. Interior architecture—History—21st century. 3. Decorative arts—Influence. I. Title. II. Title: Recrafted : interpretations of craft in contemporary architecture and interiors.
NA687.K75 2010
745.09'051—dc22   2009050615

Printed in China

www.monacellipress.com

10 9 8 7 6 5 4 3 2 1
First edition

Designed by Claudia Brandenburg, Language Arts

Cover: Hot Rod House; Tom Kundig/Olson Kundig Architects; photographs by Tim Bies/Olson Kundig Architects (front) and Benjamin Benschneider (back)

INTRODUCTION

For as long as I can remember, I've had a particular way of working. I begin by making notes based on my thoughts about a subject and my research into it. This is followed by interviews, which I record and then transcribe—a time-consuming process, but one that enables me to discover things I missed while absorbed in the original conversations. I cut the notes and transcripts into strips of paper—sometimes hundreds of them—and lay them out on the floor, arranging and rearranging them until their order represents the story I want to tell in the way I want to tell it. With a pencil and yellow pad, I draft whatever it is I'm writing, then type it up with the Olympia manual I've had for forty-plus years, rewriting and retyping until the work is done—at which point it finally goes into the computer.

While I don't work precisely this way all the time, unless I follow some variant of my routine, however cumbersome it may sometimes be, the outcome doesn't feel authentically "mine"—because it hasn't emerged from the process by which I practice the craft of writing.

As a result of this approach—and my sensitivity to when my own work becomes authentic to me—I have always been interested in why certain things feel "crafted" and others do not. In 1964, Supreme Court justice Potter Stewart famously observed that while he couldn't precisely define hard-core pornography, "I know it when I see it." That is how I feel about craft. It may seem easily discernible. But the more of it you see—the more you realize how many forms it takes, and how imaginatively it can be interpreted—the more resistant craft becomes to easy explanation.

On the one hand, everyone knows what it is: craft involves, in the architect Adam Yarinsky's formulation, "the hand and how it registers on the making of something"; an informed understanding of a (typically organic) material and how to tease out its potential; and a method of making that combines a vast store of skill-based knowledge with experience and artful intuition. Viewed from this perspective, a craft object is easy to identify: George Nakashima's tables, a glass dragonfly by René Lalique, George Ohr's pottery, a Fabergé egg.

On the other hand, this definition isn't large enough to include what we instinctively perceive to be craft when we encounter it in other, unexpected places—for example, in product and industrial design, as in the work of Tapio Wirkkala, one of the twentieth century's most prolific and versatile creators. A gifted draftsman who could express himself equally well with hand tools, Wirkkala would produce countless sketches of an object, refining his ideas with multiple models and molds. Then he would migrate this craft-based sensibility to the mass-production phase: immersing himself in the requisite processes, making design adjustments as necessary, and working side by side with the fabricators, whether the object was a Venini polychrome vase or the Finlandia vodka bottle—perhaps his best-known design, the manufacturing of which required thousands of hours of experimentation. By keeping hold of the reins throughout production, Wirkkala was able to preserve the quality of craft that had emerged during development—a quality that remained evident in the mass-produced object.

This same double vision can be applied to the presence of craft in architecture and interiors. If there is such a thing as a common understanding of "the craft of architecture," it can perhaps be found in the appropriately named Craftsman style of the architects Charles and Henry Greene—notably their 1908 Gamble House in Pasadena, California, with its superlative woodwork—or the English Arts and Crafts movement and its presiding figure, William Morris, whose own 1860 Red House featured beautifully rendered wall coverings, textiles, glasswork, and decorative painting. Yet as the twenty-five projects in this book—all of which have been completed since 2000—demonstrate, craft can take many forms and turn up in unlikely circumstances; is subject to multiple, sometimes subjective definitions; and demands reconsideration in the light of contemporary tools, materials, aesthetics, values, ways of living, and—not least—processes of creation.

Included herein are examples of traditional craft rendered via artisanal production methods, which restate historical references in a modern, sometimes ironic, context; designs that are shaped by a dialogue between the architects' aspirations and the capabilities of the makers; architects who do all or part of their own fabrication, both to invest their buildings with a personal spirit and to ensure the proper realization of their vision; projects that comment in some way on the values inherent in the idea of craft; structures that depend on a local building culture and thus promote "craft sustainability"; works that foreground industrial craft, the contributions of artists to architecture, the utility of a workshop-based approach, the tension between the hand and the machine, and the craft of pure process; and still others that employ digital fabrication to diminish the inherent distance between architecture and making. All of them, in one or another way, feel "crafted."

This is, I realize, a personal, necessarily incomplete approach to the subject. My hope is that what follows will encourage a more flexible understanding of the craft influence and how it can be used to enrich the whole of the built environment. People are drawn to handcrafted objects because the human touch invests them with individuality, personality, narrative, and authenticity. In ways both obvious and unexpected, craft can infuse the larger worlds we inhabit with those same, very welcome, qualities.

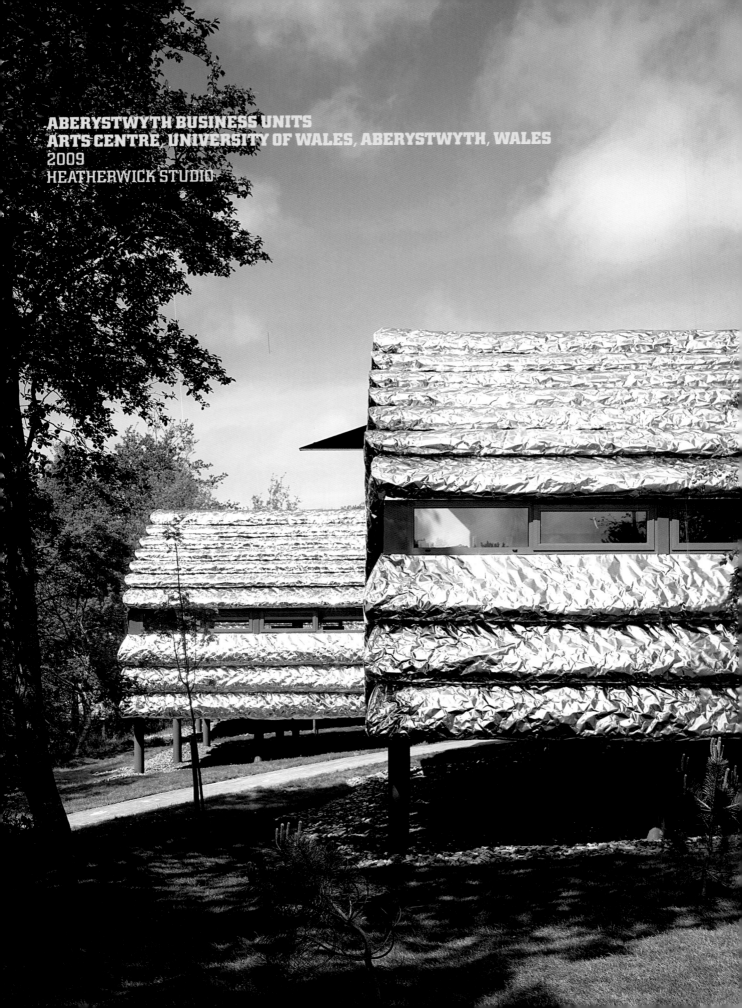

Thomas Heatherwick's design for the Aberystwyth Arts Centre at the University of Wales—eight timber-frame sheds on a wooded site, each of which accommodates two start-up arts enterprises—grew out of three impulses: to avoid what the designer calls the "big fat building" that typically houses campus cultural activities; to sit lightly on the landscape; and to control costs on the tightly budgeted project. While the basic form came easily, Heatherwick challenged himself to clad the structures in something more distinctive—and less soulless—than the usual off-the-shelf options.

Heatherwick was drawn to steel for its durability, but given pause by the expense. "You pay by weight," he explains. "So the normal thickness of, say, one and a half millimeters would have been out of our budget." Seeking an alternative, the designer discovered a rolling mill in Finland that produced steel that was fifteen times thinner—but the 0.1-millimeter-thick material dented as easily as a beer can.

"Then we thought, actually, that brings it alive," he recalls. Inspired, the creative team retreated into the Heatherwick Studio workshop and invented a crinkling device called "the Mangle," which the designer describes as resembling "a joke machine from *Chitty Chitty Bang Bang*." Cranking the sheets of steel between its dimpled rollers produced "a consistency of inconsistency"; the lack of rigidity was remedied by spraying a CFC-free insulation foam—originally meant for pig sheds—on the back of the crinkled surface. Once it hardens, says Heatherwick, "You end up with a lightweight, inexpensive, highly insulated, artistically unique cladding."

The siding was shaped on site: rolls of steel were unspooled through the Mangle, cut to length, and attached to the timber frames. The loglike appearance derives from the material's one-meter vertical dimension, and the need to curve it outward to accommodate the waterproof joints between pieces. When Heatherwick experimented with bending the steel around the building's corners, it bunched up unattractively; instead, the installers folded and matched the seams, says the designer, "like a tailor puts together a dress."

Heatherwick believes that, as the site's trees grow thicker, and the crinkled surfaces increasingly reflect their leafy surroundings, his steel log cabins will gradually disappear—"like one of the early *Predator* films," he says, "where someone can go invisible."

"The arts center is quite an eccentric one—they haven't got a narrow definition of what the arts is all about," observes Thomas Heatherwick. Given his client's flexibility and the project's restricted budget, the designer opted for eight modestly sized, single-story structures, as opposed to a "big fat building," to avoid major expenses like elevators. "The studios needed to be very simple in many ways," Heatherwick says.

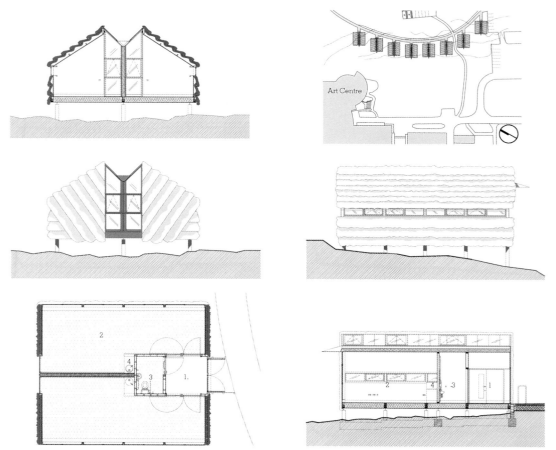

"I didn't want to overimpose a style on the creative people who were going to use the spaces," says Heatherwick of the studios' unexpectedly simple, light-filled interiors. Visual interest derives from the ultra-thin steel cladding, which was unspooled on site from what Heatherwick describes as a "giant toilet paper dispenser" and rolled through a custom-designed and -built crinkling device. The need to create waterproof seams between the steel sheets generated the curved, loglike forms.

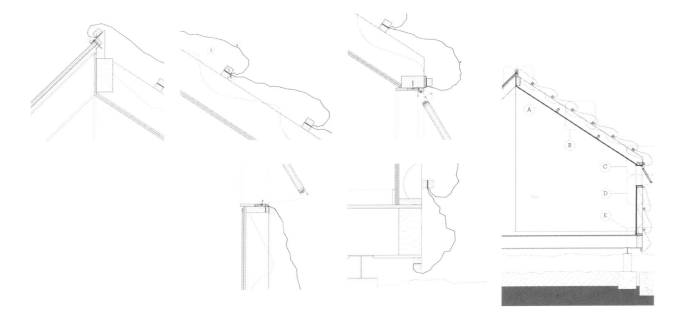

HOT ROD HOUSE
SEATTLE, WASHINGTON
2006
TOM KUNDIG/OLSON KUNDIG ARCHITECTS

"It was basically a shack," says Tom Kundig of the circa 1918 residence he "hot rodded" for his family. Kundig's many experiments included gluing massive glass panes directly into their new steel frames. "That's asking for a lawsuit if they leak, but you can do it with your own project," he says. The gaps in the ebony-stained cedar shutters, which replicate the house's original siding, were custom-cut by Kundig's carpenters.

Growing up tinkering with cars, Tom Kundig became enamored with the idea of "hot rodding"—taking a standard-issue Ford or Chevy and, through ingenuity and panache, souping it up to the point where it could feed dust to a Ferrari. Later, as an architect, Kundig found himself similarly intrigued, this time by the possibilities inherent in responding to existing conditions.

So when the architect and his wife went house-hunting in Seattle, he asked her to "find a dump that I can play with." She obliged with a dilapidated early-twentieth-century "shack." While retaining some structural elements and aesthetic eccentricities, Kundig proceeded to hot rod the house—and, in his own formulation, turned an old jalopy into the pride of the neighborhood.

While the configuration of the house is relatively straightforward—a guest suite on the ground floor, a living/kitchen/dining space above it, and a third-floor bridge connecting a family room and master suite—the architect seized every opportunity to experiment with ideas that weren't commercially viable, either to test their limits or because they struck him as "cool." Kundig's approach emerges most dramatically in the sculptural three-story stair he named "the Dragon." Constructed from steel plates and welded together on site, the object enabled the architect to explore the process of strengthening steel by bending it—and more audaciously than he had previously attempted. Kundig's appetite for risk is also evident in the house's overscaled glass panes, which he glued directly into the structural steel frame, believing that they would stay put in an earthquake.

Some inspirations emerged during the construction process, notably the decision to install the front door lock backwards, so that its moving parts would be visible. Others are purely whimsical: depending on the residents' preferences, the television can be raised or lowered, with a custom-designed hoist, between the second and third floors.

In addition to being, as its designer hoped, the acme of cool, the house is the product of what Kundig calls "cultural sustainability." Observing that craft is by nature community-based, the architect ensured that all work was executed by local carpenters and craftspeople—although, as with any hot rod, he continues to fine-tune the design as inspiration strikes.

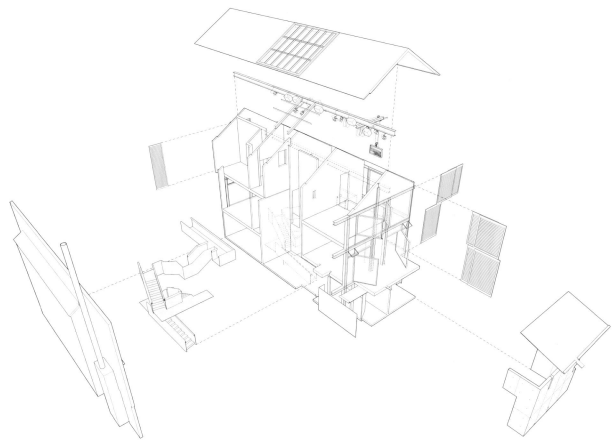

"The T-shaped opening [between the living room and kitchen] was existing," says Kundig. "That's the old trim, and I left it beat up. I wanted to save as much of the original character as made sense, then open up the interior so the house could breathe." Kundig's engineering collaborator, Phil Turner, devised the cable-collection device for the hoist that moves the television between the second and third floors.

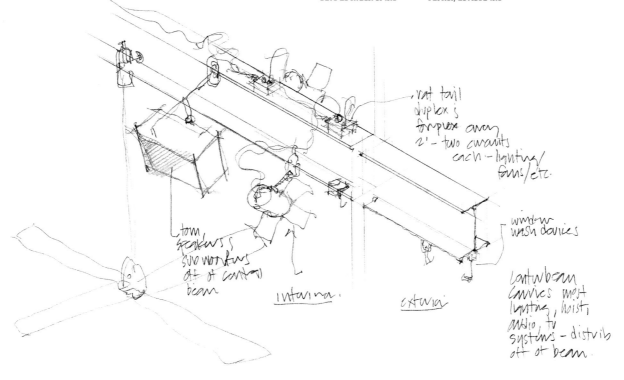

The entry door lock "changed after the drawings," Kundig recalls. "It's like sculpture—you modify because you make discoveries. I was working on the door and thinking, 'That's cool, the way it works—why not put it on backward so you can see it move?' Then I took the skin of the door and folded it into a pull." Of the many such inspirations, including the window handles, Kundig says, "Inventing it because you can invent it was the premise of the house."

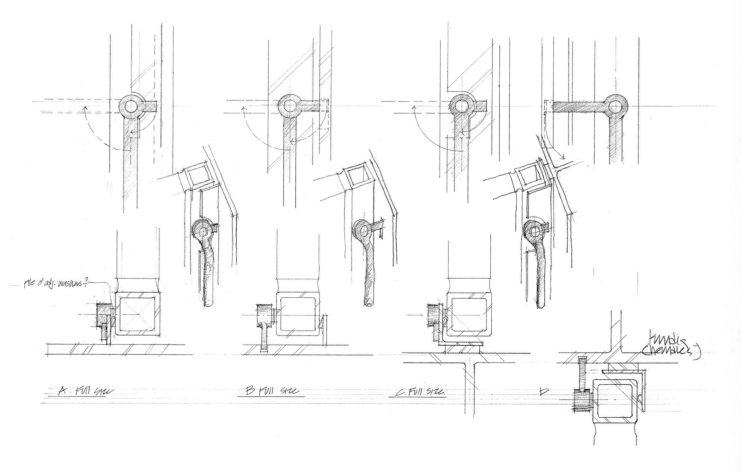

"Instead of buying art for the walls, we made craft in the building," Kundig explains. "The Dragon," the house's sculptural three-story stair, "was impossible to engineer. It's just folded metal that's welded together and holds itself up with a series of touch points as it rises. My gut told me it would stay up—I just couldn't prove it. It's idiosyncratic, it's yours, and it's personal," he adds. "That's the whole nature of craft in general."

DEFORMSCAPE
SAN FRANCISCO, CALIFORNIA
2009
FAULDERS STUDIO

Each of the individually cut and numbered tiles, which vary in size from seven inches to five feet, "is asymmetrical," says Thom Faulders. "Some of the angles were so subtle that if the placement was off by just a sixteenth of an inch, it threw everything off." Spacer plugs proved effective on the deck, "but when we got to the wall it was just unbearably difficult," the architect recalls. A full-scale paper pattern provided the solution.

The arresting look of this "outdoor room"—the rear yard of a single-family dwelling in San Francisco—evolved from architect Thom Faulders's desire to resolve two opposing impulses. Previously, the yard had featured a deck that obscured the natural slope of the terrain, which Faulders hoped to reclaim; his client, however, requested a flat, entertainment-friendly space. The architect proposed to marry the ideas with an optical illusion: a deck with a deformed grid pattern would suggest that the yard was sloping toward the base of a Japanese maple at the rear of the lot when in fact the surface would remain perfectly horizontal.

Faulders assumed the process would be a relatively straightforward matter of creating a three-dimensional pattern in the computer and printing it onto a two-dimensional template for the deck surface. In fact, the design proved frustratingly hard to resolve. The creative team had first to select a single perspectival point from which the illusion could be optimally perceived, then decide how dramatic the deformation should be: too subtle, and the effect got lost; too extreme, and the outcome was a black convergence of lines at the base of the tree. Ultimately, the architects alternated between the generative and the empirical, repeatedly tweaking the grid in the computer and testing it on a studio model.

The design finalized, the individually cut and numbered marine-grade plywood tiles that form the deck surface were attached to an understructure of fiberglass grating. The "grid lines" are actually $5/16$-inch gaps that facilitate drainage. Unlike in a rectilinear grid, however, on which maintaining straight lines is fairly simple, the difficulty of replicating the design's curves resulted in tiny miscalculations that produced large inaccuracies. While the installers were able to develop plastic pegs that served as effective spacers, the system failed on the rear wall, which projected the grid seven feet upward. A full-scale, twenty-five-by-seven-foot paper pattern provided the solution.

Faulders likens the project's evolution to the process followed by a writer or composer: envisioning an outcome and finding a way to achieve it without making the travails of the journey legible. Materiality, often at the center of craft, is absent here; rather, as with a sonnet or symphony, the craft lies in inventing a process, then erasing all evidence of it, leaving only an experience to be enjoyed.

"Normally you design a three-dimensional thing in the computer and translate it into a three-dimensional thing in the world," Faulders says of the brain-twisting design process. "Here we were going to design a three-dimensional thing that was a flat plane in the world but *looked* like a three-dimensional thing." Though the illusion is optimally perceived from a certain point—the residence's home office—the architect strove to make the pattern interesting from every perspective. His personal favorite is a side view.

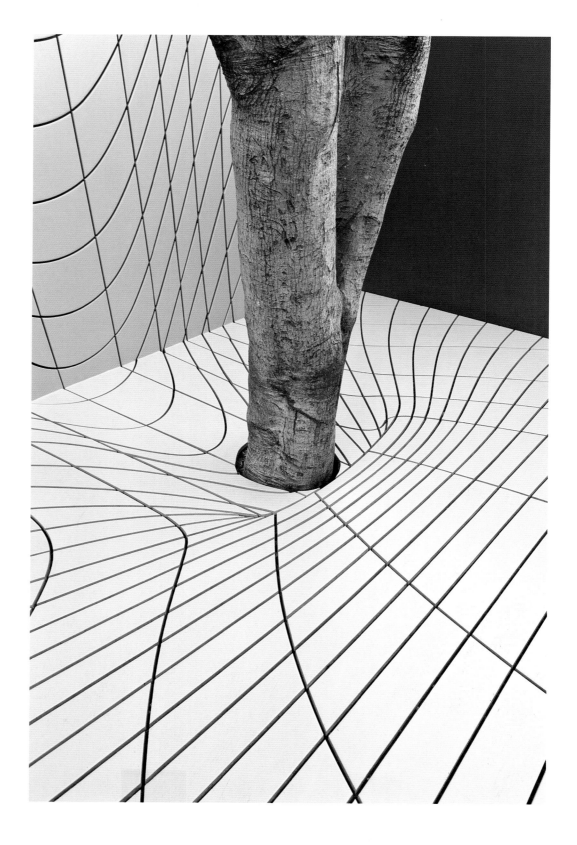

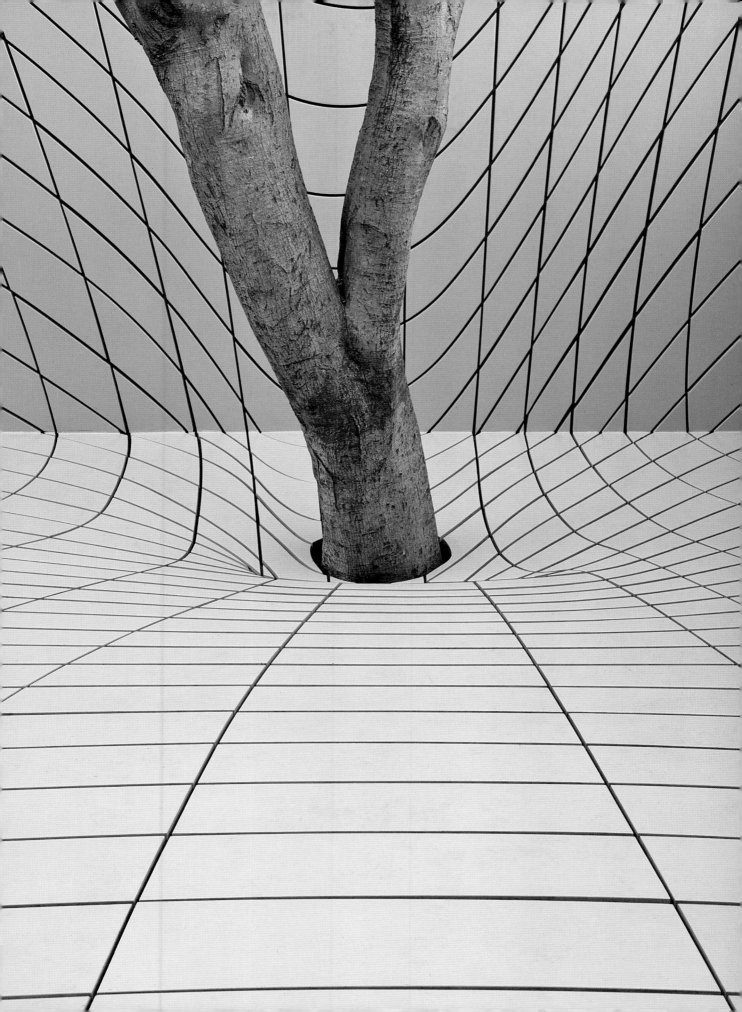

This High Renaissance–style banking hall, designed by the firm of York and
Sawyer in 1917, was acquired by the Rhode Island School of Design for use
as its new art and design library. Among the challenges of the conversion,
the most daunting was the need to create reading and study space and shelving for some 117,000 volumes in a structure that, although four times the
size of RISD's previous facility, proved insufficient to handle the program.

Architects Monica Ponce de Leon and Nader Tehrani of Office dA
responded with two freestanding structures on axis with the hall's barrel-
vaulted ceiling—a circulation island and a study pavilion—separated by a
piazza-like zone Tehrani calls "the living room." While a winged, cantilevered roof distinguishes the circulation structure, the study pavilion is
the more complex volume. Its side walls are fitted with carrels configured
for multiple body types; study and conference spaces nestle within it; tables
for individual and collective work occupy the roof; and bleachers overlook
the living room, much as a grand outdoor stair serves as a vantage point
above a plaza. Indeed, with its physical variety and multiplicity of private
and public experiences, the design, believes Tehrani, "practices a kind of
micro-urbanism."

Constructed from parts cut from medium-density fiberboard with a
CNC (computer numerical control) router, the two modules were conceived
as outsized furniture pieces. In what Tehrani describes as "a collaborative
design-build scenario," Office dA worked with a contractor from the begin-
ning to develop a scheme that could be built economically and unfussily
without compromising the architects' intentions.

Citing Henri Labrouste's nineteenth-century Bibliothèque Ste.
Geneviève as an example of traditional craft, Tehrani observes that Office
dA's digitally crafted version "acknowledges the radical economies of contemporary construction but also the cultural desire to commemorate what
libraries historically have meant." By amplifying the essence of its surroundings without mimicking its style, Office dA's classically composed installation restates the library's social significance in a modern design language.
The architects do so, moreover, via the mass customization—"multiples in
variation," says Tehrani, "rather than the multiples in repetition of mass
production"—that digital craft affords.

Apart from creating
reading and study
space and shelving
for 117,000 volumes,
Office dA's conversion
of a banking hall into
a library involved
restoring the original
structure's architec-
tural features and
making the building
code-compliant in
what Nader Tehrani
calls "a stealth way."
Because some five
hundred students live
in the building above
the bank, Tehrani
observes, "the library
was also going to
be a living room for
these people."

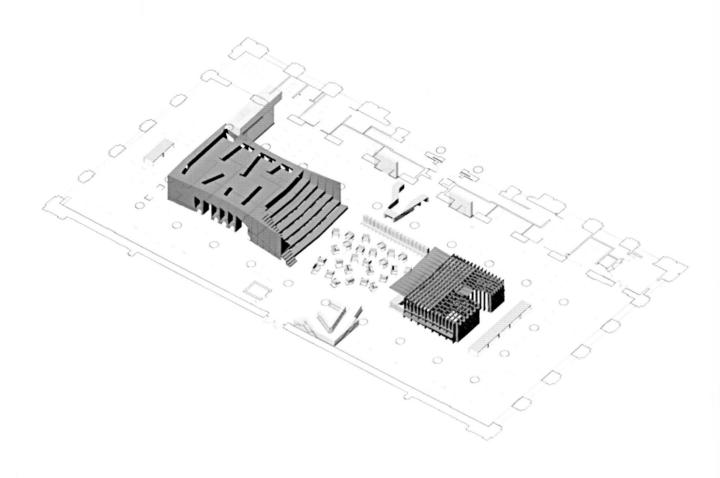

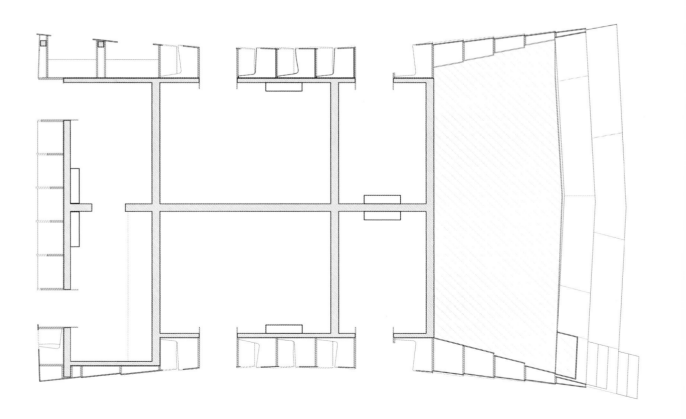

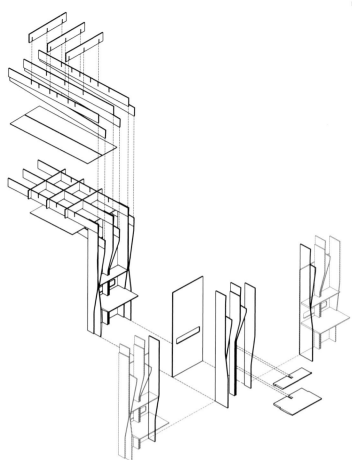

The circulation island and study pavilion were conceived as large-scale furniture pieces: each was fabricated off-site, put together for fine-tuning purposes, taken apart, then reassembled in the hall. "The whole project was built very economically," says Tehrani. "If the contractor participates from day one in a collaboration that deals with the means and methods of construction as part of the design process, you don't have the trauma of value engineering."

GOODMAN HOUSE
PINE PLAINS, NEW YORK
2004
PRESTON SCOTT COHEN

The form of this country retreat—a peaked-roof gable house that, through simplification, inflation, and a sprinkling of the surreal, upends conventional expressions of "home"—grew out of the owners' experience of summering in a converted barn. Having enjoyed that structure's high ceilings and exposed beams, the couple decided to find a barn of their own and have it disassembled and reconstructed, with a new envelope built around the original frame, on their property near the Catskill region. The pair was drawn to the traditional Dutch version with its broad, navelike central axis, side aisles, and massive H-shaped supports and purchased an example dating from the early 1800s.

In keeping with his clients' desire to retain the barn frame and open space in pristine form, architect Preston Scott Cohen left the interior largely open, locating most of the rooms in a two-story volume tucked into a side aisle. Eliminating the partitions that provide stability in a working barn provoked the architect's liveliest invention: an exposed steel frame that sits between the wooden beams and walls, bearing the wind loads and holding up the facades. Releasing the skin from its structural function also enabled Cohen's Dalí-esque scramble of forty-eight windows, which showcase interior as well as exterior views.

Like a peaked-roof gable home, an old barn comes freighted with sentimental associations; Cohen removes them from the exterior by infusing the design with playfulness and idiosyncrasy, and from the interior by enclosing a much-beloved craft object—the hand-hewn barn frame—with curtain-wall construction typically used for office buildings. Yet showcasing the frame in such a manner, Cohen observes, confronts the beholder with a "pure tectonic expression of architecture—and in a domestic setting, where it normally isn't offered." And by pairing the timbers with their contemporary craft counterpart—the hand-welded steel frame—the design establishes a pas de deux between pre- and post-industrial structure, one in which the partners contrast and harmonize with endless variety.

The seemingly random arrangement of the house's forty-eight windows—which were placed to showcase different views—"makes it impossible to identify how many levels there are, or even to tell the difference between a door and a window," says architect Preston Scott Cohen. Within, the nineteenth-century Dutch barn frame and twenty-first-century steel cage—each of which provides different support functions—converge at multiple points.

The barn frame's horizontal beams create the illusion of a lower ceiling, domesticating the space without diminishing its expansiveness. The ten-foot-square breezeway—running the structure's full width and open at both ends—serves as an interior porch and forms the main entrance. "The breezeway invites you not just to enter, but to explore the experience of entering," Cohen observes.

CASA A
VILCHES, CHILE
2008
SMILJAN RADIC

"The house had undergone a series of extensions," says Smiljan Radic. "We eliminated these and changed the way it was used to take advantage of its spatial structure." Sculptor Marcela Correa arranged some sixty massive stones on the two ramped terraces and around the property. Radic made sketches on site, tailoring them to the skills of his builders: "Not having to design was a relief—your work begins with what is at your reach."

Casa A, the rural getaway of Chilean architect Smiljan Radic and his partner, sculptor Marcela Correa, is located some three hundred kilometers south of Santiago, at the confluence of an oak forest, a nature preserve, and the foothills of the Cordillera Mountains. After visiting the simple and traditional 1960s-era cabin for nearly two decades (it belongs to Correa's family), the couple decided to redesign it to better suit their needs and aesthetic predilections.

Radic eliminated a series of extensions, returning the house to its original form, and—with the addition of oversize sliding doors—opened the stripped-bare interior to a pair of new terraces and, beyond them, the forest. He also added a widow's walk to capture views of the Cordilleras, South America's Rocky Mountains.

The architect frequently collaborates with Correa, whose work, he says, "can range from locating a piece on a site to direct participation in architectonic decisions." In this instance, Correa placed some sixty massive stones on and around the property to produce, as Radic explains, "a continuous artifact. Casa A and the rock garden have the same environmental weight—they create a single atmosphere." Indeed, the severe, iconoclastic arrangement of architecture and sculpture—which is entirely off the grid, sustained by solar panels, spring water, and a fireplace—seems closer to an art installation than a residence.

Since the house developed partly in response to what local workmen could produce, Radic eschewed conventional plans, preferring to design on site with the tools at hand, an experience he found liberating. The outlines of the terraces, the architect says, "do not correspond to pre-positioned geometries. They emerged from simple issues like avoiding trees, following the natural terrain, and so forth." The craftwork he describes as "poor—not the result of an ancient tradition. It works on the limits of insecurity, with the freedom to measure different phenomena of a construction in an empirical manner, and promotes error as something reasonable."

On the other hand, in defense of his unskilled builders, Radic observes that their work "may, paradoxically, be called 'state-of-the-art technology' as very few people can execute it."

"From what we know, the workmen had never built structures of this complexity," says Radic of the house's imperfect yet effective carpentry. Though the architect let the laborers' talents influence the outcome—his principal formal choice was to whiten the interior—work on the spare, simple residence required seven months to complete, in part because of Radic's infrequent site visits.

An interior designer is often characterized as a "decorator"—someone who selects furnishings, fabrics, and accessories and installs them in rooms. As this triplex apartment in an Art Deco building overlooking New York's East River demonstrates, the designer's role is considerably more comprehensive. The spaces do indeed contain vintage pieces by famous names. Yet virtually everything else in the residence, which was created by William Sofield, was custom designed and treated and meticulously handcrafted.

The design begins not at the walls but behind them, with the insertion of contemporary cooling systems. To integrate the vents into the architecture, Sofield designed cast-bronze grilles, based on a pattern in the building lobby, to cover them. Elsewhere, when masonry was removed from the spiral stair to open up views, copies of the original iron balustrades were fabricated to fill the spaces.

Every wall received careful treatment: Swedish wax, Venetian plaster, hand-rubbed lacquer, pigmented varnish. Floors were ebonized, and bookshelves lacquered black over red, giving them a distinctive glow. Every room was fitted with a different custom-designed, cast-bronze doorknob; when a bathroom required a sink, one was hand-carved from marble.

Draperies, wall coverings, and carpets are similarly singular, a gambit that reaches its apogee in the oval-shaped salon. There Sofield's motif for the painted-and-gilded gaufraged leather paneling reappears in the curtains and rug, a layering he likens to "an old Paris hotel, where there's one pattern and it's on everything."

Sofield also designed many of the furnishings, including some with flexible functions, and commissioned different artisans to execute others. And certain pieces are slipcovered or changed entirely twice a year—in spring and fall—so that rooms remain seasonally appropriate.

As the designer puts it, "Anything worth doing is worth overdoing." Yet considering every detail of an interior invests the entirety with elegance and spirit—and at the heart of this lies the indelible contribution of craft. Such a project involves hundreds of artisans of every sort, each contributing to the outcome, a process Sofield likens to a tennis game. "I bring things to the table, the people making them volunteer different ideas, and the result is a new vision," he says, "a complete synthesis of everyone's talent." *That* is more than decoration.

The curving sofa in the salon, custom designed by William Sofield, can be divided into two sections; upholstery is changed seasonally. Artist Nancy Lorenz created the burnished silver-leaf panel that conceals the television in the dining room's lounge area. Custom-embroidered drapery by Gianluca Berardi of Macondo Silks screens a grille in the living room; the cast-bronze piece, inspired by a design in the lobby, conceals an HVAC vent.

In the library, says Sofield, "we lacquered the bookshelves red and then blackened over them so as to give them a special glow." In the stairwell, Sofield removed structural elements and replicated the original railing—featuring a distinctive brass "horse" detail by William Bottomley, the building's architect—to replace them. The oculus above the stair was added during the renovation.

"There's no room for error," says Sofield of the custom-cut mirroring—with separate steel fabrication—in the master bathroom; the bronze fixtures for the marble sinks were handmade by P.E. Guerin. In the master bedroom, Sofield designed the Louis XVI—style beech bed and the Rateau embroidery motif on the silk faille headboard and coverlet. According to the designer, multiple teams can work on such an object—"a frame maker, a gilder, a carver, the people who weave the fabric, then the ones who embroider the fabric."

INI ANI COFFEE SHOP
NEW YORK, NEW YORK
2004
LEWIS.TSURUMAKI.LEWIS

Between 2002 and 2005 Lewis.Tsurumaki.Lewis completed a series of restaurant projects that might be characterized as "semi-design-build." While leaving the bulk of construction to a contractor, architects David Lewis, Paul Lewis, and Marc Tsurumaki personally undertook the fabrication and installation of the signature elements of each design, the better to preserve their quality and craftsmanship.

For Ini Ani, a 350-square-foot coffee shop on Manhattan's Lower East Side, LTL responded to the owners' requirement for two programs within the tiny space—a to-go component and a lounge area—by, in Tsurumaki's formulation, "producing the shop itself out of the components of the cardboard coffee cup." This translated into a circulation route from the entrance to the service counter defined by a "lid wall"—lined with 479 plaster casts of takeout coffee cup lids—and a semi-enclosed box within the larger box of the shop, constructed principally from two-inch-wide strips of cardboard, that forms the lounge.

In their workshop, the architects fabricated a frame for the box of cold-rolled steel, which they assembled and installed on site; the 25,000-odd cardboard strips, procured from a distributor, were then hand-cut to fit the varying widths of the frame and pressed into place. LTL also designed and built simple chandeliers, decorative shelving, and furniture using the same steel members.

For the wall, the trio drilled holes into sheets of medium-density fiberboard, inserted into them plaster casts of the multiple lids they had found, then skim-coated and painted the MDF to produce a single monolith. The wall proves effective at different scales: at a remove, it plays as a rhythmic pattern; up close, the variety of lids offers the fascination of a butterfly collection.

The firm's choice to handcraft the project's major elements affected the outcome in multiple ways. It enabled the architects to realize a distinctive project quickly and inexpensively (three months, $40,000). It generated the design, which evolved from the tools and materials with which the makers were conversant. And it let LTL produce a true work of architecture— one that privileged material and surface—in a situation in which the usual opportunities afforded by plan, volume, and form were severely limited.

Everything below the horizontal datum line formed by the top of the banquette was built by a contractor; everything above— notably the box within a box of cardboard and steel—was personally fabricated by David Lewis, Paul Lewis, and Marc Tsurumaki. The coffee shop's design was in large measure shaped by what the architects could make in their studio and the materials and tools with which they were conversant.

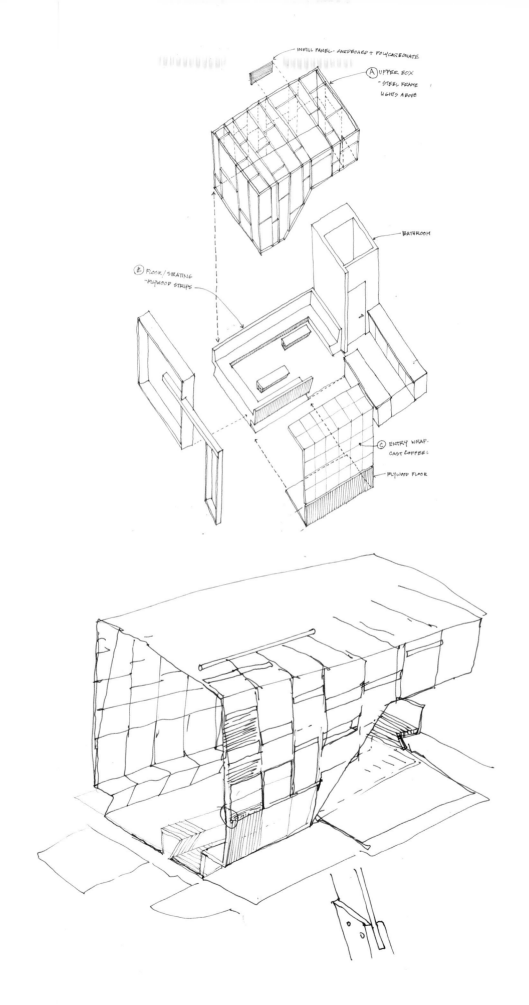

INFILL PANEL - CARDBOARD + POLYCARBONATE

(A) UPPER BOX
- STEEL FRAME
LIGHTS ABOVE

BATHROOM

(B) FLOOR / SEATING
- PLYWOOD STRIPS

(C) ENTRY WRAP -
CAST CONCRETE

PLYWOOD FLOOR

While the steel components of Ini Ani's front door and street-front window were cut in a fabrication shop, the architects designed and built the sign, attaching the letters with screws. LTL's original plan was to make the "lid wall" out of cast-plaster tiles; when that approach proved prohibitively heavy, the architects inserted plaster casts of takeout coffee cup lids into sheets of medium-density fiberboard, then skim-coated the entire surface to produce a uniform effect.

HOTEL SEEKO'O
BORDEAUX, FRANCE
2008
ATELIER D'ARCHITECTURE KING KONG

The architects
anchored the
structure on its corner
lot—directly across
the quai from the
Garonne River—by
aligning the windows
with those of the
neighboring buildings
and by tilting back
the facades along a
line that begins at
the cornice adjacent
to the northern face,
then slopes downward,
turns the corner, and
terminates at the
cornice of the shorter
structure on the
hotel's eastern side.

Bordeaux is justly celebrated for its centuries-long architectural heritage.
Yet since the election of Mayor Alain Juppé in 1995, the city has witnessed
substantive urbanistic changes, notably the redevelopment of the Garonne
River's once-industrial left bank into a pedestrian-friendly esplanade and the
introduction of an elegant tram system that has united the historic center
and outlying districts into a single metropolis.

Thus, when the locally based Atelier d'Architecture King Kong was
engaged to design a hotel for the Bacalan district, at the end of a row of pic-
turesque eighteenth- and nineteenth-century structures along the Garonne,
the firm sensed an opportunity to challenge the city's aesthetic traditional-
ism. With Bacalan, a down-at-the-heels industrial area, about to undergo
major transformation as part of Juppé's redevelopment plan, King Kong
sought to create a design that would contrast with the district's prevailing
style and avoid the usual contextualizing approach of architectural pastiche.

The Seeko'o—a snow-white, origami-like structure whose name means
"iceberg" in Inuit—accomplishes this by erasing the rectilinear patterns
of stone-and-mortar construction that remain the hallmark of the hotel's
neighbors and Bordeaux's most ubiquitous manifestation of craft. In place
of the stonemason's handiwork, King Kong substituted a 10,700-square-foot
facade composed entirely of white Corian, the first such use of DuPont's
solid-surface acrylic polymer. The resulting enigmatic abstraction—smooth-
surfaced, virtually seamless, and baldly synthetic—opposes the hegemony of
the city's aesthetic past by opposing, in a way that is both mischievous and
sublime, the craft tradition that produced it.

Ironically, the scheme's formal rejection of historic craft required
that King Kong embrace its contemporary variant. Cladding a building in
Corian for the first time—expanding the material's possibilities—demanded
skill and imagination from all participants. The 5.5-meter-high, half-inch-
thick panels were exactingly cut by a digitally controlled machine tool;
DuPont's designers developed brackets that could be hung on rails attached
to the Seeko'o's concrete substructure; the rails themselves were designed
to absorb panel dilation and keep the skin perfectly flat; and the installers
glued together the curving, tongue-and-groove edges and sanded the panels
to a satiny finish—a final artisanal flourish.

Despite the hotel's aggressively modern appearance, Bordeaux's city hall, which authorizes construction, embraced the design after rejecting a number of more conventionally conceptual schemes developed by the owners' original architects. "The city wanted to bring energy to this area," explains Atelier d'Architecture King Kong principal Paul Marion. "This creates a link to the past and is an expression of what we do today."

MOBILE CHAPLET
FARGO, NORTH DAKOTA
2006
MOORHEAD & MOORHEAD

Granger and Robert Moorhead's Mobile Chaplet features two canopies of black-coated thermoplastic composite rods; the exterior layer supports the outer edge of a horseshoe-shaped bench that measures approximately fourteen inches at its deepest and the interior layer performs the same function on the inner edge. What the Moorheads describe as a non-denominational space of reflection was completed for a modest $20,000.

Inspired by the sublime interconnection of architecture and painting at the Rothko Chapel in Houston, the North Dakota artist Marjorie Schlossman commissioned six architects to design what she described as "chaplets": small, movable structures, each incorporating Schlossman's site-specific paintings, that might serve as non-denominational spaces for reflection.

Whereas five of the chaplets must be taken apart and reconstructed, the team of Granger and Robert Moorhead (in collaboration with their architect father, Richard) chose to create an object that would itself be mobile. The result is a modern-day version of the horse-drawn covered wagon that helped settle the American West: an eight-by-sixteen-foot trailer bed covered by two canopies woven from approximately 230 thirty-foot-long thermoplastic composite rods. A horseshoe-shaped plywood structure serves as a bench and also holds the canopies in place; each rod rises from a hole on one side of the trailer, passes upward through the plywood, then comes down through it again into a hole on the other side. (Small metal collars secure the rods to the trailer and float just beneath the bench to keep it from slipping downward). Schlossman's contribution is a mural painted directly on the chaplet's "floor."

The object's simple, evocative form arose from the Moorheads' intent to create a sense of place without resorting to the confining rib-and-membrane design of the original covered wagon. The two canopies, which touch at their fourteen-foot apex but do not otherwise inter-lace, arose from the brothers' memory of making baskets as Boy Scouts; accordingly, each layer was woven by the three Moorheads, in traditional over-and-under style, over several days, an experience the brothers liken to "an architectural father-and-sons fishing trip." The nested forms provide the requisite visual density, support both the inner and outer edges of the bench—and, by evoking both the timeless values of hand-making and the windswept North Dakota fields, imbue a contemplative space with the soul of humankind and the spirit of nature.

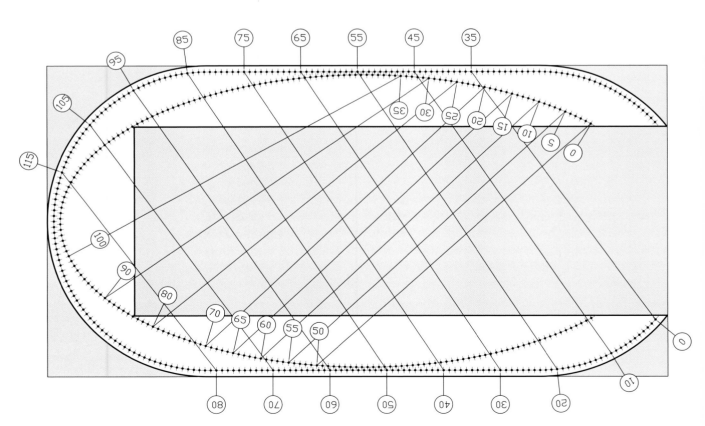

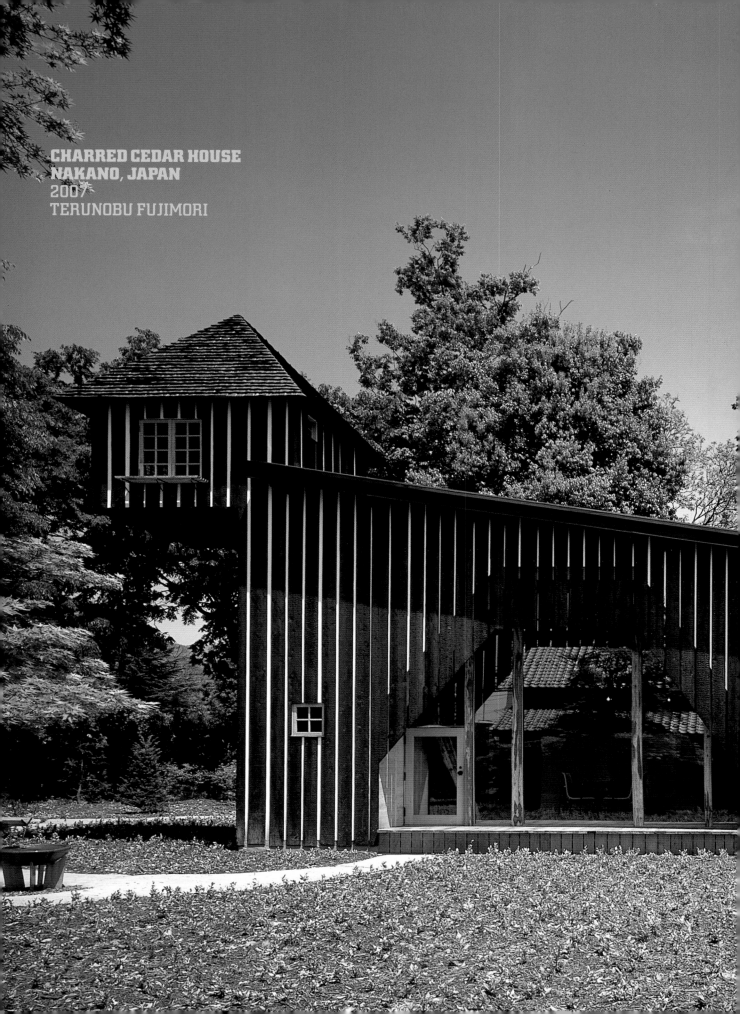

CHARRED CEDAR HOUSE
NAKANO, JAPAN
2007
TERUNOBU FUJIMORI

The architecture of Terunobu Fujimori is often described as strongly connected to nature and primitive building forms on the one hand and as playful on the other. Both characterizations are accurate. Yet neither quite captures the special personality of Fujimori's work, which derives not only from his eccentric, sometimes perilous-looking designs but also from his thoughtful consideration of organic materials and the unusually hands-on way he treats them.

The owner of this property engaged Fujimori to design a residence that would at once preserve its centuries-old greenery and water features and nestle organically within them. While initially flummoxed, the architect eventually found his inspiration while exploring a cave dwelling on a visit to see the famed murals at Lascaux, France. The notion of a single cavernous space evolved into the double-height living/dining/kitchen area that forms the heart of the design; the glass of the front facade, held in place by rough-hewn beams, seems to disappear as night falls and light fills the interior, heightening the sense of natural shelter. Wanting a timber that was "strong but tender," Fujimori settled on Japanese chestnut for the floor, walls, and ceiling, treating the boards with a sanding machine to create an appropriately textured finish.

The house takes its name, as well as its nearly reptilian appearance, from the charred cedar boards that constitute its cladding. A traditional method of defending against decay—carbonizing the surface makes the wood less perishable—the craft was typically applied to boards of under two meters; in this case, working with a team of friends and colleagues, Fujimori charred some four hundred boards of approximately eight meters in length, finishing the labor-intensive task in a day. Though the planks warped, the architect turned this to aesthetic advantage, filling the gaps between the blistered wood with smooth white plaster.

Fujimori defines craft, succinctly, as "handmade," and indeed the notion of multiple hands—his own among them—contributing to a project remains indispensable to his work. Among the most "natural" and "primitive" of impulses is the creation of shelter. By doing so collectively, via the application of craft, the architect invests each of his buildings with an embracing, and unmistakably human, spirit.

Terunobu Fujimori describes the roof of the Charred Cedar House as resembling "the deck of a mother ship." Of the three tops of hinoki cypress "growing" above it, says the architect, "Whenever I put free-standing columns I cannot resist piercing them through the roof." Fujimori's penchant for the perilous appears in the tearoom perched on the upper edge of the house's western facade. Access is via ladder through a panel in the living room wall.

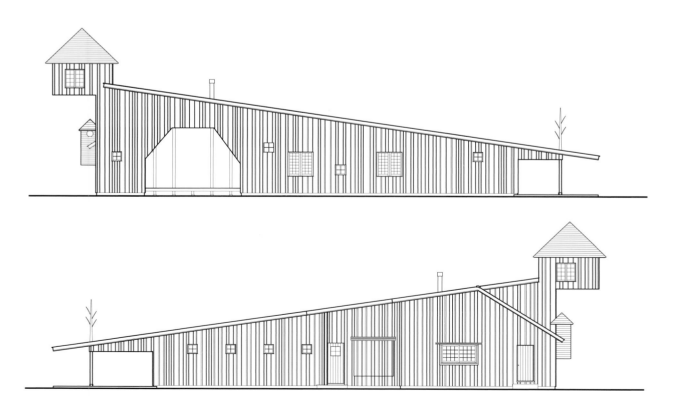

The pathway leading through the garden to the house is formed from a mudlike mortar with a brushstroke finish developed by the architect. To amplify the sense of a natural environment within the main living space, Fujimori cut down a mulberry tree and shaved off the bark to fashion a pillar for the kitchen. The architect also pasted bits of charcoal to the plaster surface of the hearth: "Fire is necessary for a cave," he explains.

MOLORI SAFARI LODGE
MADIKWE GAME PRESERVE, SOUTH AFRICA
2008
KIRK LAZARUS WITH STEPHEN FALCKE

Craft traditions aren't typically associated with wealthy businessmen and their luxury retreats. Molori Safari Lodge, nine kilometers south of the Botswana border in South Africa's 185,000-acre Madikwe Game Preserve, represents an exception. The modest-looking outpost—principally eight thatched-roof structures on a low rise—was developed by the Johannesburg-based tycoons Kirk Lazarus and Ivor Ichikowitz, initially as a friends-and-family getaway, then as an ultra-exclusive resort offering twice-daily game drives along with the usual pampering. While Ichikowitz, who acquired the property, originally modeled it on a nearby safari lodge (there are about thirty throughout Madikwe), Lazarus stepped in during construction and began a demolish-and-redo regimen with the builder, finding the look he wished for through trial and error.

The outcome stands in contrast to what designer Stephen Falcke, who collaborated on some of the interiors, calls "the dark-leather-and-stone, more 'African' look" of most such properties. Molori's five suites (four of them free-standing) feature soaring exposed-thatch ceilings, open-plan living/sleeping/bathing layouts, and floor-to-ceiling glass walls that completely fold away, opening the interiors to private decks and pools, with views across a 24,000-acre plain to the Rand van Tweedepoort hills.

Lazarus characterizes Molori's style as "Afro International," which has an ominously Austin Powers ring to it. In fact, the lodge is notably lacking in pretension, owing in large measure to the strata of craftwork embedded in its construction. The decorative ground was applied by two local artisans—a woodworker, who built the countertops, tables, doors, accent pieces, and headboards from indigenous leadwood trees, and an ironsmith, responsible for the balustrades, stair rails, and fireplace detailing. Over this was layered more finished wood-, stone-, and tilework, by offices in Cape Town and Johannesburg; rooms were detailed with vernacular examples of craft from Mexico and Asia as well as Africa. Into this mix, Lazarus introduced distinctive pieces that individualize each space—a hand-beaded Ethiopian armchair, antique Chinese cabinets, mokoro (dugout canoes)—and finally high-end furnishings, including work by Marcel Wanders and Philippe Starck.

The end product is surprisingly graceful. The lodge is not a kitschy mix of the primitive and lavish but rather a well-judged alchemy of local, national, and global craft.

While the more finished fabrication at Molori Safari Lodge was executed by offices in Cape Town and Johannesburg—notably BA Shopfitters, which completed the millwork—various artisans detailed the eight thatched-roof main structures. A local smith, Danie Roberts, forged the ironwork, including the balustrades, which resemble branches and vines. Lucas Mabele—who subsequently became the lodge's barman—designed and hand-set the river-stone patterns in the floors.

Willie Delport, a local farmer and woodworker, used indigenous leadwood —so named for its thousand-kilogram-per-square-meter weight—to craft Molori's distinctive countertops, table bases, doors, head-boards, and accent pieces. Many of the lodge's objects are vernacular examples of craftwork. Others are not as they appear: the chandelier in the main lodge, seemingly African in origin, was in fact composed of wicker floor lamps from the Belgian company Sempre.

TANNER STUDIOLO
NEW YORK, NEW YORK
2002
RICK JORDAN

Completed in 1476, the Gubbio studiolo was the private study of Federico da Montefeltro, duke of Urbino. A Renaissance masterpiece of perspectival intarsia, the studiolo's cabinets reveal, through partly open latticework doors, objects representing the duke's interests and history. What is remarkable is that the sixteen-by-twelve-foot room is an illusion—a trompe l'oeil executed not in paint but in thousands of pieces of wood inlay.

In 1997, Michael Tanner, a Manhattan physician, saw the studiolo in its new home, the Metropolitan Museum of Art, and decided to re-create it in the reception area of his living room, filling the cabinets with artifacts reflecting his own life and interests. He and his wife engaged Rick Jordan, an artist specializing in interiors based on elements drawn from different artworks, and the trio developed a scheme that included four principal and four secondary cabinets. For the frieze, they chose a quotation from the philosopher Epictetus: "Appearances to the mind are of four kinds. Things either are what they appear to be; or they neither are, nor appear to be; or they are, and do not appear to be; or they are not, yet appear to be." Tanner liked the observation because it encapsulated the four diagnostic possibilities: true positive, true negative, false negative, and false positive. He then reworked Epictetus's next sentence to read: "Rightly to distinguish between the Real, the Not, the Occult, and the Illusory is the task of the wise man." Each of the main cabinets illustrates one of these concepts, while the secondary ones display familial, musical, and astrological objects.

Fittingly, the multiyear project resembled a collaboration between royal patrons and a court artisan. As Jordan painted the cabinet structure, he and the Tanners struggled with what to put in them; once objects were selected, the artist executed a template for each cabinet, which his clients then critiqued. Eventually, the project outgrew both the reception area and the original concept: Jordan brought in the twentieth century by painting Albers-esque squares on the remaining walls and borrowed the ceiling from a painting by Giotto—of a painted ceiling.

The mix is unlikely. But it coalesced into a room as evocative as the original, and as nearly a remarkable expression of craft: a trompe l'oeil painting of a trompe l'oeil executed in wood chips—a double illusion.

In the Real cabinet, the rock refers to Samuel Johnson; in response to Bishop George Berkeley's assertion that reality was an illusion, Johnson kicked a stone and—feeling the pain—said, "I refute it thus." A modern-day echo appears in the baseball and can of Kiwi, which recall the moment in the 1969 World Series when Cleon Jones proved he'd been hit in the foot by a pitch by indicating the shoe polish on the ball. The typewritten page in the Household cabinet is from the novel *Auntie Mame*, written by Tanner's father, Patrick Dennis; the French Zig Zag corkscrew belonged to Tanner's parents.

The Illusory cabinet is comprised of visual impossibilities, including a mirror that reveals a unicorn in the living room. In the Science cabinet, the telescope is a replica of Sir Isaac Newton's. The binoculars in the Family cabinet refer to Tanner's love of bird-watching, the mortar and pestle to his wife Mary Anne's career as a biochemist. The Music cabinet includes a phrase from the Beach Boys' "Good Vibrations," with the numerical frequencies—the vibrations—standing in for the notes.

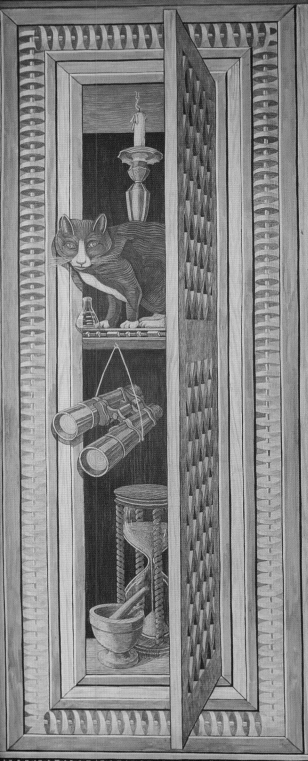

COURTYARD HOUSE
TORONTO, CANADA
2008
STUDIO JUNCTION

Architects Christine Ho Ping Kong and Peter Tan inserted their Toronto residence into a former industrial building. The adjacent vacant lot is now an enclosed courtyard, which also contains a studio. Because the neighborhood, near the junction of two railroad lines, is urban-industrial, the pair eliminated conventional windows, admitting natural illumination into much of the interior by excavating a glazed "cutout" from the second floor. "The longitudinal section reveals how the light comes in," says Tan.

Most people would have seen a thirty-by-forty-foot concrete-block warehouse and an adjoining vacant lot in an industrial neighborhood in Toronto. Architects Christine Ho Ping Kong and Peter Tan of Studio Junction, however, saw their future home. The couple envisioned a residence that looked inward, rather than onto the street, across a walled outdoor space to a studio—a courtyard house like the ones they had visited in India and Latin America and at Pompeii.

The pair demolished the concrete-block facade facing the lot (which they enclosed and landscaped) and set about inserting a house into what remained. Inspired by Louis Kahn and Tadao Ando—architects, Tan says, "who use light as their main medium"—they developed strategies for internalizing the outdoors. The most effective is the second-floor "cutout," a terrace with banks of windows that bring natural light into the first-floor kitchen, second-floor bathroom and hallway, and double-height office.

To maximize the play of light on the clean geometries of the house's volumes—and to preserve the purity of their vision affordably—Ho Ping Kong and Tan built it largely by themselves, drawing on Tan's years of woodworking experience to craft the interiors all but entirely from wood. Using predominantly mahogany and variegated teak plywoods, Tan deployed his skills to shape modernist forms at once pure in their near-total absence of distraction (doors, cabinetry, and hardware are suppressed) and remarkable in their warmth, surface animation, and material richness. The pair also used craft to differentiate between old and new by wrapping the entry in cedar—a grace note, in a sea of concrete block, signaling the presence of a home.

The residence also celebrates craft for craft's sake, as with the sliding doors on the office cabinetry—elegant thin slats selected from off-cuts compiled during the five years of construction. And the project enabled Tan to expand his skills, with elements like the drawers for shoe storage tucked into the lower three stairs.

Citing the effort invested in the cedar-lined entry volume, as well as the screenlike courtyard gate, Ho Ping Kong suggests another value of on-display craftsmanship: it demonstrates "concern and inhabitation." Particularly in what both architects describe as a neglected neighborhood, such evidence of care amounts to a small but significant example of community building.

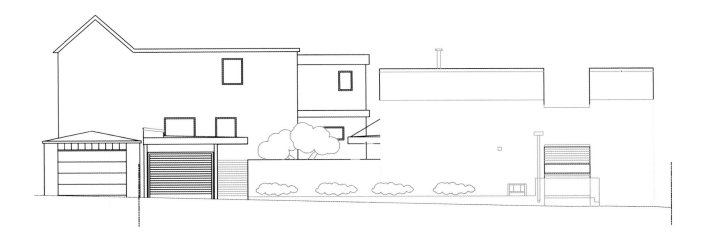

The architects wrapped the entry, directly below the terrace and facing a public street, in cedar to create a clear distinction between the industrial concrete-block shell and the warmth of the home within. Tan also took pains to craft a latticework courtyard gate. "In a neglected neighborhood, these things show that extreme care has been taken," he says. "A lot of people don't believe it's a house, and we wanted to have these moments where they would do a double-take."

The office, children's areas, and stair called on different aspects of Tan's woodworking skills. The thin slats on the faces of the office cabinetry were fashioned from construction off-cuts; many of the strips of knotty Douglas fir lining the kids' rooms were reclaimed from the original building's roof truss; and the drawers tucked into the lower stairs remind people to remove their shoes before ascending.

LING LOFT
NEW YORK, NEW YORK
2001
DAVID LING

"I wanted to make it my own world," says architect David Ling of the loft, in a nineteenth-century former industrial building, in which he lives and works. That meant not only expressing his fascination with water and light but creating polarities: between the colorful and monochrome, rectilinear and curved, wet and dry, and most of all between the loft's hand-built structure and the industrially produced materials it contains.

Ling separated the three primary functions—living, working, and sleeping—with water, light, and space. The architect positioned the office on the street, dividing it from the living area with a "moat"—a pit excavated from the basement and bridged by posts reclaimed from the original structure—in which a perimeter of water surrounds a platform furnished with a conference table and chaise. Beyond the main living space, which is washed with light from three skylights and a row of windows, Ling inserted a "pond," its bottom covered with black stones. Wooden blocks in the water form a path to a stair, which leads to a second-floor sleeping loft; from beneath the bed—which cantilevers over the space below, a grown-up version of a hanging cradle—a waterfall cascades, replenishing the pond.

Essential to Ling's conception is "the dichotomy between 'delivered by a factory and crafted by hand'"; thus, whenever possible, industrial materials were exposed to "a human intervention, to retake ownership from the machine." The acrylic-mirror flooring received an abrasive circular sanding, and the most eccentric object—a curvilinear, galvanized-steel cone that bridges the two floors and serves as a hanging chair below and a shower enclosure above—was created by Ling and his builder on site. The living area's eighteen-foot-long concrete kitchen volume derived its "baby-butt" smoothness from the fabricator's inability to produce the finish Ling requested (necessitating multiple sandings). And when he realized he couldn't afford to install a waterfall on the rear wall, says Ling, "I decided I'd go for metaphor," engaging the artists Loye & Derrickson to layer multiple coats of ultramarine blue and black over the bricks.

"There are different levels of craft," Ling says of the design. "There's the crafting of the space, to have the requisite level of tension—the opposition between elements. And then the crafting of materials and details, to support what the space is doing."

"There's a gradation of function that flows from public to private," says David Ling of the main floor of his loft, which measures one hundred by twenty-three feet. The forty-foot-long office is set on the street; the moat—a pit excavated from the basement—is both library and meeting space; the main living area, which contains the kitchen island, is largely residential but used periodically to display models and samples; and the pool contains a stair that leads to a second-floor master suite.

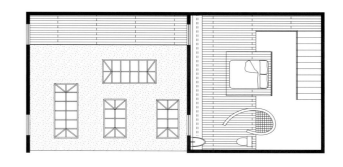

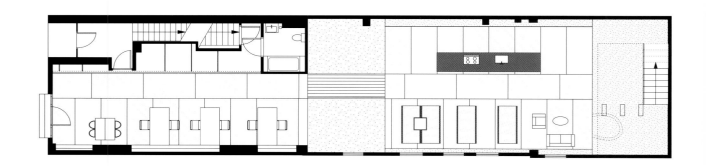

The space's most unusual object is a sculptural cone, wrapped in galvanized steel, that bridges the two floors; it functions as a hanging chair below and a shower enclosure above. For Ling, the form "captures the dialogue between organic and geometric, straight and curved, metallic and rustic." The architect and his builder worked out the shape and construction of the object on site.

For this Chicago house, Dan Wheeler's clients requested a warm, intimate retreat that could, on occasion, accommodate gatherings of more than two hundred people. The architect describes his firm's response as both introverted and extroverted. Above, a nearly windowless box encloses the private quarters; these spaces look inward toward transparent light courts, open to the sky, which bring rain, snow, and sunshine into the interior. The first floor, conversely, is glass enclosed and can be opened almost entirely to the garden.

The family had previously lived in a nineteenth-century residence; just as that structure had been representative of its time, Wheeler's clients explained, they wanted their new home to be a snapshot of what architecture and the building trades could achieve in the early twenty-first century. The firm answered their desire by aiming for a level of performance well beyond the norm for a private dwelling.

Appropriately for world-class art collectors, the innovative structure is museum quality. Since the second floor features forty-foot concrete cantilevers, the architects and engineers worked to ensure that long-term deflection—that is, sagging—wouldn't exceed three-quarters of an inch. To keep out Chicago's winters, four-inch pultruded fiberglass beams (with no conductivity) were attached to the building, aerated autoclave concrete panels (with good insulation value) set on top of them, and closed-cell foam sprayed into the resulting gap. For the first floor, the team spent six months developing mullions for the double-layered glass that were sufficiently airtight to prevent cold-air leakage and condensation. To keep even slight deflection from impacting on the curtain wall, the massive glass sliding doors were suspended from steel beams.

In keeping with the desire for warmth of another sort, bronze was selected as the metal of choice; five manufacturers produced the window frames and doors, door handles, stair and decorative panels, floor diffusers, and chimney cladding that give the house its richness. Like the bronze, wood and stone finishes were treated to emphasize their materiality; French limestone floors received a wire-brush scouring prior to honing, producing an easily cleaned surface that feels natural beneath the feet.

While many of the material treatments and structural systems required bespoke solutions, it is the whole, in Wheeler's view, that represents the project's truest expression of craft—"not just one thing in itself, but how everything comes together," he says. "That's the craft of architecture."

Bronze components, including the window frames and stair panels, imbue the house with warmth and richness; the distinctive fence, also crafted from bronze, permits views into the garden while screening major public rooms. "We could have used stainless steel, but that was too white and too corporate," says Dan Wheeler. "We chose bronze because it's self-healing, and it weathers over time. The idea was that the exterior would age and have a patina, and the interior would be kept pristine."

"Since the floor was stone, to allow the indoor/outdoor expression, and the walls were glass, it was potentially an acoustical nightmare. So the ceiling was done in wood, to absorb sound," Wheeler explains. The thermal movement of the second-floor exterior insulation was uniform, so plasterers were able to apply an outer layer of custom-pigmented stucco to expanses exceeding an unprecedented two hundred square feet without perceptible cracking.

TURTLE CREEK WATER WORKS
DALLAS, TEXAS
2002
D.I.R.T. STUDIO

"What is in some ways
hard to appreciate,"
Julie Bargmann
observes, "is how such
a tiny site can have
such a sublime scale.
To have such extreme
changes in elevation
is great—not only in
the landscape, from
the bluff down to the
creek, but from the
pumphouse down to
the tank. The tanks
are twenty feet deep,
and the tank walls
are so high that you
can't see into them
unless you're on the
pumphouse roof."

Julie Bargmann has what she calls "a reservation about preservation." A landscape architect whose D.I.R.T. Studio is known for repurposing industrial sites without erasing their history, Bargmann nonetheless remains resistant to embalming the past. Rather, her work foregrounds the significant historic elements of a site while permitting them to continue to age and evolve. The challenge, she observes, is to use restraint—"to look hard at what to leave alone, what to amplify, what to suppress, and what to recraft."

Restraint drove Bargmann's reinvention of a former waterworks—a pumphouse and two twenty-foot-deep concrete reservoirs—on the edge of a deep ravine in the Highland Park district of Dallas; the owner conceived of the property as both a fund-raising venue and a family garden. Attracted to the site's dramatic changes in grade and the impact of nature on a modern ruin, Bargmann chose to let planting "colonize" the areas around the pumphouse and "to protect the voidness of the tanks."

The architect "pulled the landscape of the ravine up to the pumphouse like a blanket" to replicate a sense of natural overgrowth. Concrete slabs were broken up and used for path pavers in the gardens; preexisting plumbing was configured to create a waterfall that cascades from the garden level into the larger of the reservoirs, a feature operated by the waterworks' original pump handle.

"Celebrating the emptiness" of the reservoirs required multiple strategies. Painting done by the water department to denote tank levels was cleaned of graffiti and preserved intact. Several inches of water, fed by a length of pipe, cover the floor of the smaller reservoir, reflecting the sky and filling the space with a gentle echo. A border along the edges of a new slab in the larger reservoir allows native grasses to flourish; a crack in the floor that had been opened by vegetation was enlarged into an island of sumac. Most important, in the architect's view, is the procession into the empty space: a ramp draws visitors downward between the tank wall and a new restroom/storage volume, withholding the full revelation of the void until the last step.

The outcome is a thoughtful commingling of present and past environments: a contemporary social space imbued with the spirit of a working landscape in which, in Bargmann's view, "pure pragmatism becomes poetic."

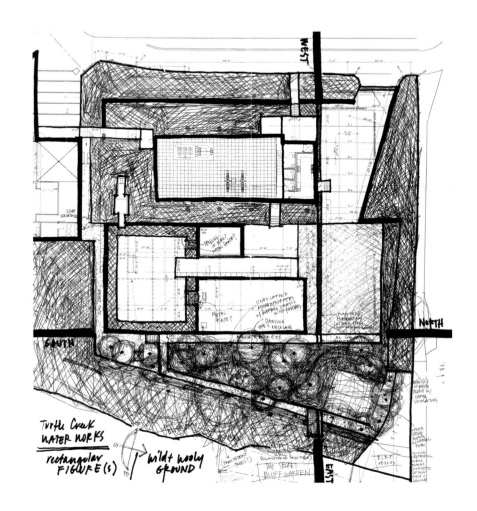

Turtle Creek
WATER WORKS

rectangular
FIGURE(s)

wild wooly
GROUND

"We took the plumbing that was there and replumbed it into recirculating fountains," notes Bargmann. "What I always say about these industrial sites is that I couldn't design anything better. The question is, how do you work with such a place? Partly it's willful preservation, but it's also recognizing that it's fine the way it is—respecting its previous life and letting it continue to age, instead of objectifying or fetishizing it."

VILLA FOR AN INDUSTRIALIST
SHENZHEN, CHINA
2009
STUDIO METASUS, PETER LYNCH (STUDIO THEM), AND AHLAIYA YUNG

Though the upper
floors are distin-
guished by an array of
domes, on the ground
floor Peter Lynch and
Ahlaiya Yung opted
for curving walls
finished in green and
white high-relief
slip-cast ceramic
tiles. "The pattern is
a simple grid until
you get to the coves,
which are curved in
two directions," says
Lynch. "We couldn't
lay a grid pattern
on it, so we drew
the location of every
tile and the workers
installed them."
Lynch and Yung used
skim-coated plywood
forms to convert
structural columns
into abstract "trees."

Twelve courses—216 holes—make Mission Hills, in Shenzhen, "the world's No. 1 golfing community," according
to its promotional material. Benefiting from policies that turned Shenzhen into China's first Special Economic
Zone, Mission Hills also markets lavish villas in which "the grace of Tuscan forms combines with Hawaiian
architectural themes."

Whatever that might mean, it stops—as New York architect Peter Lynch and his local partner, fashion
designer Ahlaiya Yung, discovered—at the front door. Engaged to design a villa's interiors, the pair found rooms utterly
devoid of everything but structure, the sellers having assumed that the buyers would hire their own decorators.

Rather than replicating the exterior's strange hybrid, Lynch and Yung took as a model the Ducal Palace in
Urbino. "Not fancy," Lynch explains, "just a tile floor, white walls, and elaborate ceilings." Influenced by the biologist
D'Arcy Thompson's 1917 book *On Growth and Form*, they foresaw the villa's decorative elements as echoing the non-
repetitive, self-structuring forms found in nature.

Lynch and Yung observed that, unlike in the United States, where cabinetmakers, metalworkers, and
other trades comprise an artisanal level between traditional craftwork and industrial production, no such middle
zone exists in China. The pair hoped to transcend this, says Lynch, by "inviting factories to do low-volume, detailed
work, and craftspeople and contractors to extend their range."

This strategy produced a sequence of ceiling installations—in Lynch's formulation, "meditations on pattern and ornament"—that evolved from a back-and-forth between the designers' intentions and the makers' attempts
to realize them. The work is various and original. A latticework structure of anodized aluminum and steel, which
spans the vestibule, was arranged by the contractor's team to resemble an array of fallen pine needles. The lower
elevator lobby features a jellyfish-like dome made from rubber balls and hundreds of wooden blocks that were handmade on site. Woven rattan panels in the dining room—dimpled, says Lynch, like an ocean's surface—were created by
basket makers. The transparent bell in the upper elevator lobby, seemingly arrested in mid-toll, is in fact a collapsible object crafted almost entirely from identical wood spindles.

Lynch admits that, in certain instances, and despite multiple attempts, the craftwork fell short of expec-
tations. But having coaxed the makers out of their comfort zones, he had to honor their efforts. "Craft," he says, "is a
negotiation—not a dictation."

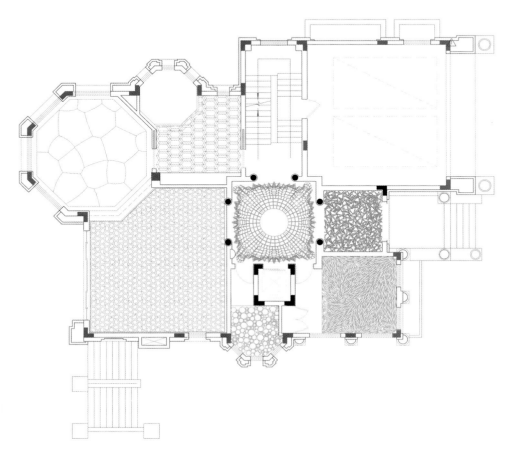

A ghostly latticework bell, constructed from wood slats and brass fasteners, is suspended in the upper elevator lobby and library and "makes a space where there otherwise wouldn't be one," says Lynch. "It's a collapsible structure, like an expandable crib. You assemble it and pull it up and it moves from being a cylinder to being a parabolic dome." As with the jellyfish-like dome in the lower elevator lobby, the structure was crafted and assembled on site.

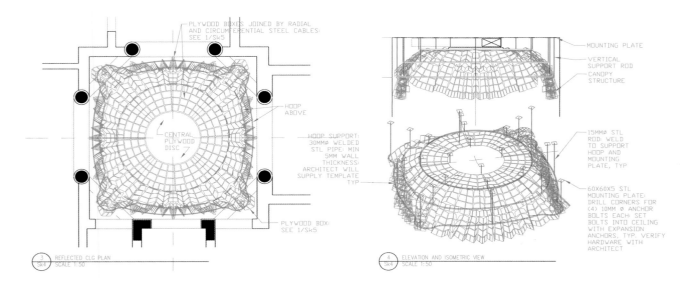

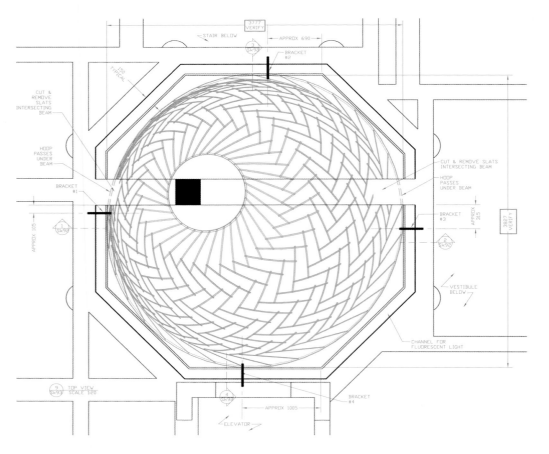

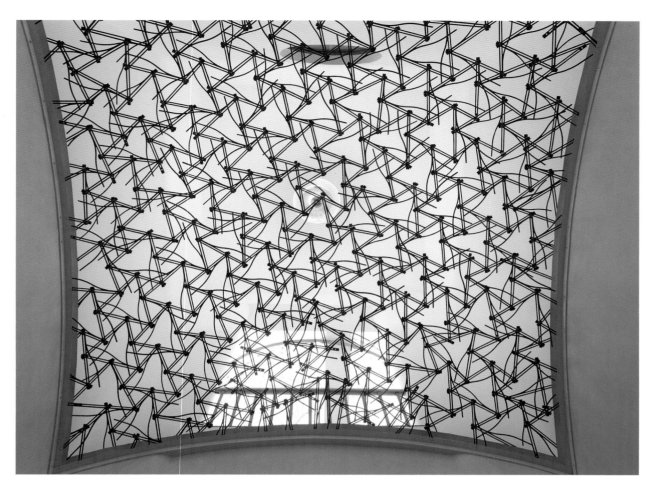

"The villa didn't have to be coherent from space to space, but each space needed to be coherent itself," says Lynch of the design, which he likens to a series of symphonic movements expressing a single theme.

Accordingly, rattan panels on the ceiling of the dining room, which were woven by basketmakers and stitched together, give way in the living room to a honeycomb formed by two layers of elliptical wood lattices constructed from hundreds of identical bowtie-shaped elements. The anodized aluminum "pine needle" dome in the vestibule is likewise composed of numerous identical components.

Utilitarian park buildings—concession stands, restrooms, equipment facilities, and the like—typically receive a level of design attention commensurate with their status. In Santa Monica, however, where parks are scarce and demand is high, such structures get a heavy workout and, consequently, more scrutiny. Commissioned by the city to create an architectural language appropriate to the circumstances, the local firm Daly Genik tasked itself with designing park buildings that could remain low profile yet visually distinctive—in Kevin Daly's words, "singular yet identical"—and as quick and inexpensive to erect as prefabricated structures, but without looking conspicuously "prefab."

Although the architects, mindful of the wear-and-tear factor, quickly settled on masonry, they were concerned that the concrete-block option would be not only insufficiently innovative but time-consuming to build. As an alternative, Daly Genik produced designs that could be constructed from precast-concrete building panels. Limiting the number of panels per building and detailing them offsite ensured that they could be hoisted into place and assembled with a minimum of equipment and manpower.

The firm discovered a Los Angeles manufacturer that had developed a clip system that enabled a conventional steel-stud building frame to be attached to a two-inch-thick, high-strength concrete shell during the casting process. Then the design team created a custom mold, with a rib pattern that appeared and disappeared, as though water were flowing over it, into which the concrete could be poured. This gave visual and tactile distinction to structures that, Daly admits, might otherwise have appeared "dumpy and undersized." Moreover, each of the resulting eight buildings was assembled in less than a day.

"One of the notions inherent in craft is the capacity to address a material's characteristics and extract the best from it," Daly observes. While this understanding is typically applied to organic matter like wood, it pertains here to the project's signature material. High-strength concrete requires a sophisticated mixing of ingredients and great care to pour; according to Daly, the fabricators achieved a high level of accuracy and consistency with a thoroughness that extended to special bracing of the gently curving molds so that they didn't crack or deform.

The project typifies the bulk of architectural practice: an unglamorous commission, in which the designers invested the utmost intelligence and creativity, brought to fruition by the exceptional craft of the fabricators.

The eight building types can be assembled from component parts —ranging in number from five to twelve— in less than a day. Mid-State Precast of Corcoran, California, fabricated the panels. "We started with the premise that we should not displace any park space, so all the roofs were supposed to be green," recalls Kevin Daly. "But the maintenance people couldn't imagine having a planted roof you didn't have to drag a lawn mower onto, so it didn't happen."

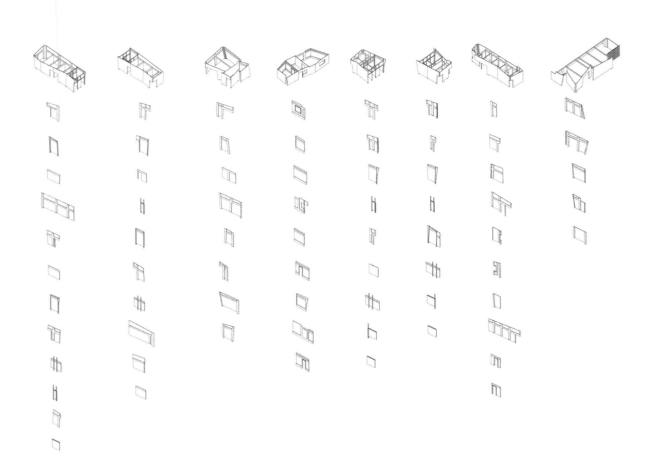

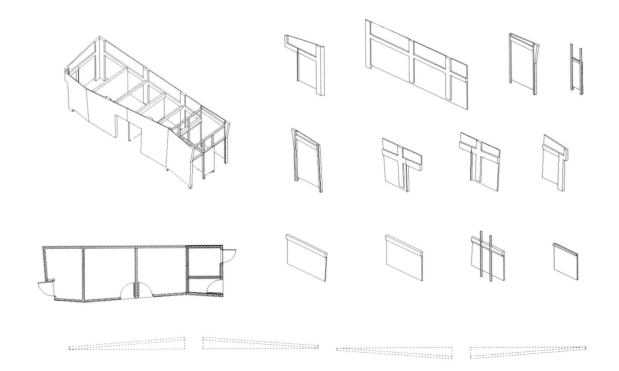

The architects distinguished the park buildings by warping the panels to create a slight hyperbolic curve and by developing a waterfall-like design that became part of the molds into which the concrete was poured. "We ended up with twenty-five running feet of unique pattern," Daly recalls. In addition to the precast-concrete structures, Daly Genik also designed announcers' booths built from durable, graffiti-resistant synthetic timber.

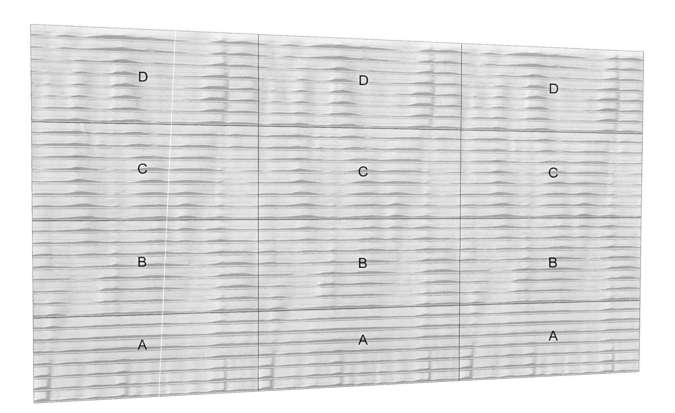

VENTANA HOUSE
TUCSON, ARIZONA
2008
RICK JOY ARCHITECTS

Rick Joy minimized the impact of the Ventana House on the desert landscape by tucking the concrete-clad ground floor behind the site's vegetation and wrapping the upper story—with a thirty-foot kitchen cantilever on one end and a twenty-foot guest suite cantilever on the other—in weathered ten-gauge steel that reads, from a distance, as a shadow cast by the Santa Catalina Mountains. "The level of craft and refinement is nearly perfect," Joy says of the steelwork.

Architect Rick Joy has characterized this residence in Ventana Canyon as being "like Clint Eastwood, up on a cliff, squinting under his cowboy hat back at Tucson." Although he's referring to its narrow band of windows (and their CinemaScopic view), the house does command its site with an Eastwood-esque reserve. Rather than constructing retaining walls, Joy located the family's private quarters in a first-floor core—barely visible behind the desert flora—and cantilevered the expansive public rooms and guest suite out over it in a strongly horizontal second-floor volume that seems to float among the cactus. While this helped maintain the delicate ecology of the site, Joy also endeavored to preserve its physical beauty by making the upper story seem to disappear. A steel wrap, weathered and rust-streaked, reads from a distance as a long brown shadow.

Essential to the success of this strategy is the handling of the material. Joy points out that "when it comes to carpentry, you can show up on a job site and get by"—he himself was a carpenter—but that steelwork requires a wealth of knowledge. (A case in point: The architect's experience building his own projects, notably the Desert Nomad House—an arrangement of three steel boxes—taught him that ten-gauge, just under an eighth-inch thick, "is the thinnest steel I know that, even with the desert temperature swings, remains perfectly flat.") The men shaping and assembling the three-hundred-odd pieces of ten-gauge that comprise this house, Joy observes, possessed both the requisite skill and the ability to treat the material with care and refinement. "Even just lining up the bluish half-inch circles of the weld marks with the screw patterns—that level of craft makes a huge difference."

The architect also valued the concrete fabricators. "Tadao Ando would have rejected them," he says of the imperfections in the exterior walls. "But if rocks fall next to the edge of the form when they're pouring, or the creamy stuff doesn't get all the way to the base and there are voids, that doesn't bother me. I appreciate the revelation of the process."

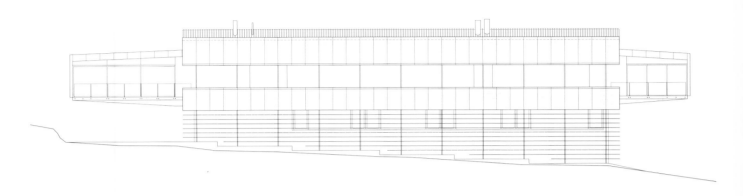

The house's porous design opens it to Ventana Canyon on one side and a panoramic view of Tucson on the other. "When it comes to steel, there's a lot of science involved in the welding and cutting," Joy observes. "You can't build anything without understanding coefficients of expansion and contraction and how much force is going to be on the weld you're going to make. If the wind is blowing, you're going to need more gas and less oxygen. You can't fake welding—you have to know what you're doing."

In 2000, the New York firm Architecture Research Office received a grant
to investigate the relationship between CAD/CAM technology and craft.
Believing that the availability of digitally controlled laser cutters had col-
lapsed the distance between thinking and making in architecture—enabling
practitioners to develop an informed intuition about materials and fabrication methods more typically associated with craftspeople—ARO principals
Stephen Cassell and Adam Yarinsky studied the impact of the variables
inherent in laser cutting (pulses per inch, power, and speed) on sheets of
paper. The project culminated with the freestanding Paper Wall, created for
a gallery installation, which exhibited surprising qualities of color, texture,
and translucency.

Several years later, a couple who had seen the Paper Wall engaged
the partners to remodel their apartment, in a landmark building overlooking Central Park, to express similar qualities. Since the program called for
converting the traditional layout into a semi-open plan loft, the architects
demolished a number of existing walls and inserted seventeen stationary
and movable laser-cut latticework screens in the entry, living/dining area,
and master suite. These at once unite the apartment's various zones and
maximize spatial flexibility.

While paper was unsuitable for permanent structure, ARO achieved
an effect comparable to the Paper Wall with a no less quotidian material: medium-density fiberboard. Experimenting in their office workshop
using a computer-controlled router, the architects developed a design that
extracted depth and vitality from the $5/8$-inch-thick boards. Part of the firm's
research involved studying the passage of light through perforated material; drawing on this, they concentrated the density of the screen openings
at two different eye levels—standing and seated—to produce moments of
greater transparency.

Observing that the traditional definition of craft "has to do with the
hand and how it registers on the making of something," Yarinsky defines
the parallel in ARO's machine-based interpretation as "the opportunity
to discover things through design—the unexpected possibilities that arise
from the way in which something is created." The outcome, says the architect, "is not just a formal exercise, but a moment-to-moment experience of
space, light, and material—one especially suited to domestic architecture,
because it gets better as you live with it."

ARO used seventeen screens to convert a conventional two-bedroom apartment into a flexible loft; LED fixtures embedded in the ceiling animate the screens' surfaces by night. The design, observes Adam Yarinsky, "is grounded in prior research that employed a computer-controlled laser cutter to transform ordinary materials, like paper and cardboard, into highly expressive elements with unexpected qualities of translucency and texture. The screens alter one's view, but also change with one's viewpoint."

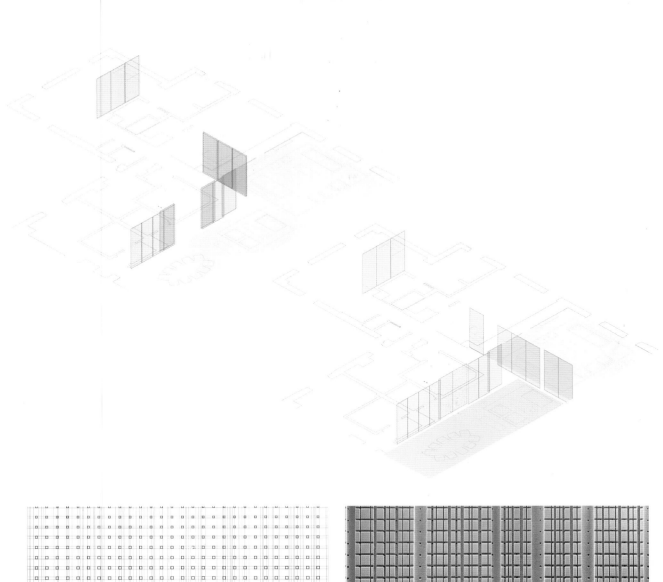

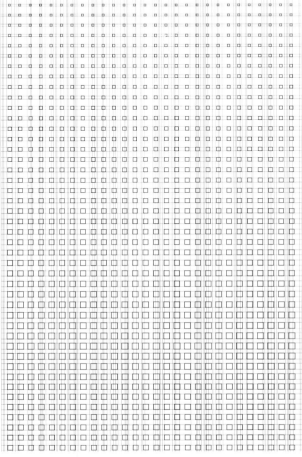

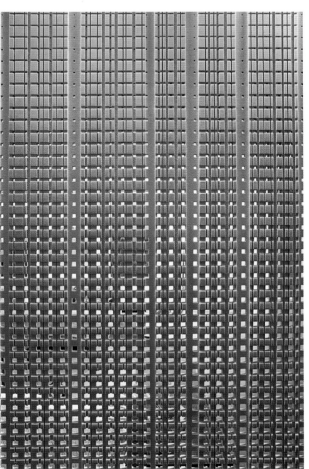

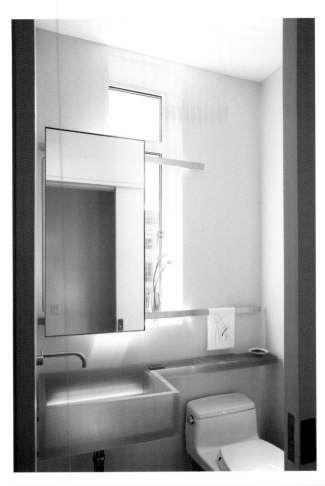

The cast-resin powder room sink represents, says Yarinsky, "an experiment involving the unexpected quality of translucency in a massive thing. It's backlit with a recessed LED—a nightlight that's integral with the architecture. The color is an homage to Neutrogena soap."

Extensive use was made of sustainable materials and finishes throughout the apartment, including FSC-certified wood and flooring, low-VOC sealants, formaldehyde-free fiberboard, and locally fabricated concrete countertops.

INTEGRAL HOUSE
TORONTO, CANADA
2008
SHIM-SUTCLIFFE ARCHITECTS

The Integral House, created for a mathematician with a passion for music, takes its name from the S-shaped integral sign in calculus, which resembles the sound hole of a violin. This expression of the owner's dual interests is not merely symbolic: the house is meant to be both a place to live and also a venue for musical performances. The notion of integration is also central to Brigitte Shim and Howard Sutcliffe's design, which draws together different ideas, influences, and elements into a comprehensive whole.

The governing influence is the curve, which the client asked Shim and Sutcliffe to explore. The architects found their response in the site. Though the house seems, on approach, to be a two-story urban residence, it transforms upon entry into a five-story structure that, actually and architecturally, leaves the city and flows downward into a forested ravine. This transformation occurs in the double-height living/performance area, which is enclosed by an undulating wall. As it moves outward into the space above the ravine, the wall dissolves into a series of oak-clad fins angled to shape multiple views. From above, the exterior is all but obscured; at the lower level, the fins open like a wooden curtain, and the house embraces the landscape.

At every scale, the structure reveals a refinement of material, detail, and craftsmanship that derives both from the architects' collaborative approach and from the local building culture. In polyglot Toronto, according to Shim, construction is as much a byproduct of multiculturalism as the cuisine. The result is an extensive network of fabricators capable of delivering a high level of bespoke work in all media. "If you can imagine it," observes Shim, "you can get it built." This phenomenon also delivers choice. Since every fin was a complicated, differently shaped sandwich of oak, plywood, and steel, the architects requested that each fabricator bidding on the job build a sample so they could judge its quality.

Multiple variants of craft appear throughout the residence. The bronze balustrades are wrapped in hand-stretched and -stitched leather. Artist Mimi Gellman encased the stair in a liner of mouth-blown glass shingles that gradually shades from light to dark blue as it descends. And Shim and Sutcliffe used digital technology to transform their own craft objects, notably the clay door-handle models, into three-dimensional printouts that served as the molds for bronze casting.

Asked by their mathematician client to explore the concept of curvature—in calculus, the computation of the area of a curved region requires the use of integrals (hence the house's name)—the architects discovered their idea in the site, which begins at an urban street and slopes steeply into one of Toronto's lushly wooded ravines. The structure makes a comparable transformation via its double-height living/performance space, which is enclosed by an undulating wall that flows outward into the ravine and seems to hover over it, suspended between the worlds of humanity and nature.

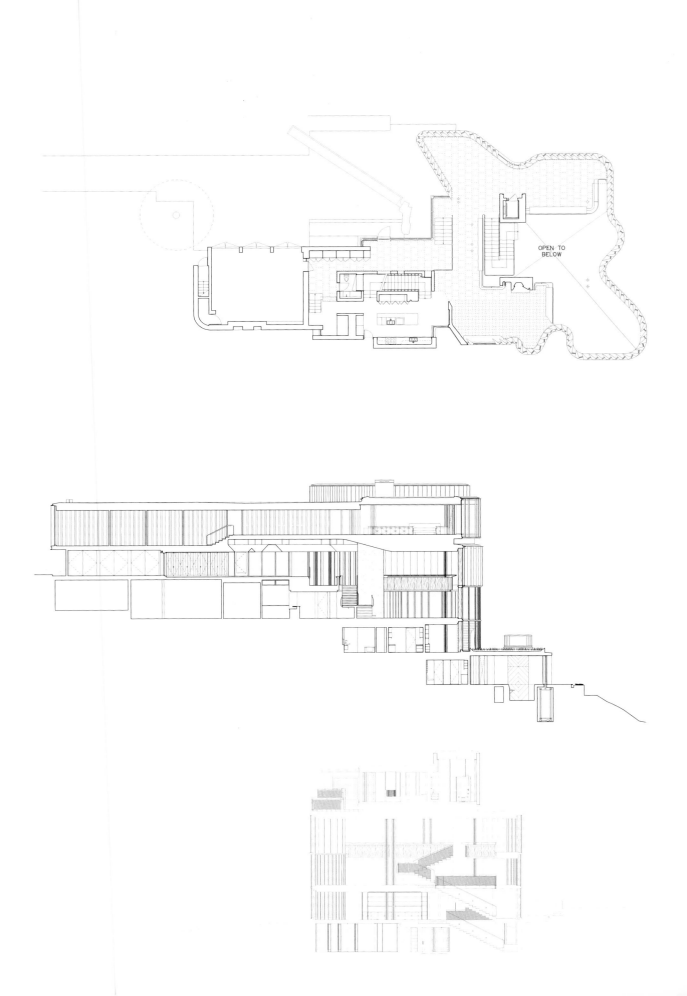

OPEN TO
BELOW

Believing that, as Shim has written, "a common understanding of what is important at each stage of construction is essential" on each project, the architects "start by learning about the local construction culture and seeking out the best craftsmen in the area." The value of this approach is demonstrated not only in the creation of the fins—which, combined with the curving line of the perimeter, shape views outward and through the exterior space back into the house—but in each of the house's finely crafted details.

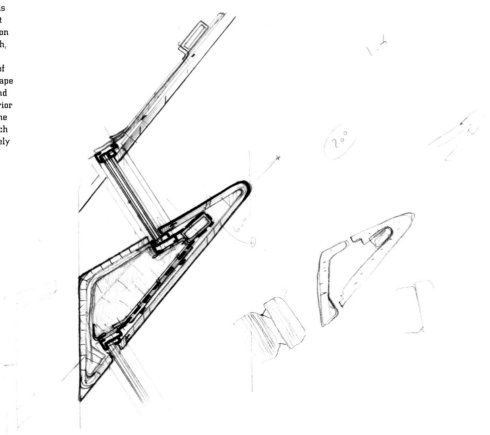

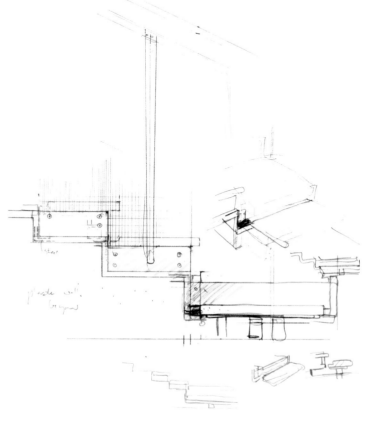

In response to the client's desire for a site-specific piece, the architects collaborated with the glass artist Mimi Gellman to create a liner that encases the stair in glass shingles. Suspended from stainless-steel cables with cast-bronze clips that resemble musical notes, the shingles gradually shade from light to dark blue. Gellman worked with craftspeople in Nova Scotia to blow and laminate what Shim describes as "a blue glass world, lit from a skylight above, that you enter."

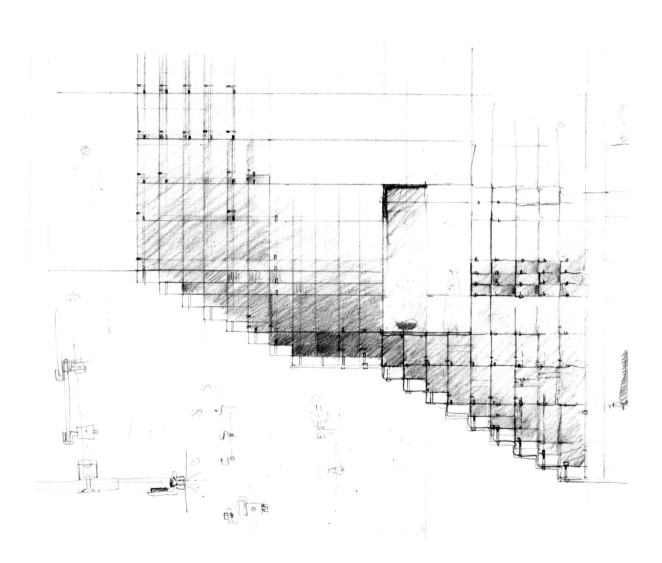

OASIS ADVERTISING
NEW YORK, NEW YORK
2004
SPECHT HARPMAN

Louise Harpman
and Scott Specht
drew inspiration for
the blue elements
they created for a loft
office from the ice
cube trays at K-Mart.
"Most people would
never look there for
an idea about craft or
making," Harpman

observes. "However,
if you open your
thinking, and start
to understand how
manufacturing or
industrial processes
work, you see evidence
of a highly specific,
beautifully designed
set of decisions."

"Craft is usually about evidence of the physical hand in the unique object," says Louise Harpman, who with partner Scott Specht designed this loft office for a New York advertising agency. "But there's evidence of the hand in mass-produced objects as well, if you know how to look for it." Industrial design—creating a particular product and making choices regarding material and fabrication that will enable it to be produced—"involves just as much craft, but it conforms to other protocols, which have to do with mechanical or industrial processes," Harpman says. For this project, the architects introduced such examples of mass-produced craft into the larger context of the craft of architecture.

Harpman and Specht took their cues from both the neighborhood—Manhattan's still-gritty Garment District, its streets thronging with rack-pushers and rattled by truck traffic—and the space itself, the top floor of a manufacturing/showroom building. To enclose a semiprivate work area, the architects constructed dividers from the off-the-shelf metal exhaust louvers seen in the windows of sweatshops throughout the neighborhood. (That the loft was itself almost certainly once a sweatshop heightens the gesture's effectiveness.) The pair also turned to the quotidian for the pendant light fixtures, inserting bulbs into cylinder-shaped air filters designed for trucks.

The architects hoped to use molds made from ice cube trays to construct the blue walls that constitute the most prominent element of the scheme: though there's nothing specifically "Garment District" about ice trays, Harpman and Specht remain partial to them, and so settled for the fact that they can be purchased at a nearby K-Mart. Unable to create a clean mold from the genuine article, however—"it's perfect for ice cubes, but not good if you want to make a tray from a tray," Harpman admits—they designed a new module based on a tray's exterior dimensions and had the requisite number fabricated in fiberglass by a boat-building concern.

"Architecture has, on one level, a refined palette," Harpman observes. Reusing the readymade in unexpected ways and circumstances "helps to expand what's considered appropriate, or even tasteful, for the profession—and expand our thinking about craft and making."

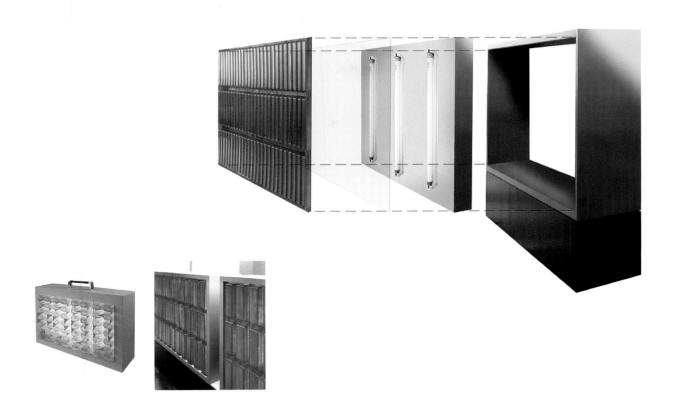

The architects incorporated a number of off-the-shelf products into the design, including cylinder-shaped air filters designed for trucks and the metal exhaust louvers that appear in sweatshop windows throughout New York's Garment District. Specht and Harpman lightly divided desk stations within the open-plan work area with a series of cork-finished "tongues." Perimeter spaces, often devoted to executive offices, here provide light and views to most workspaces.

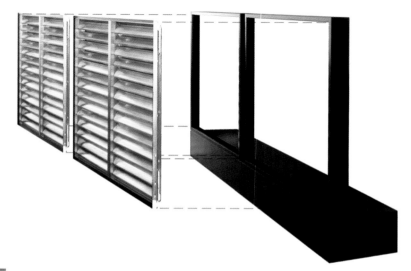

BLOOMFIELD HILLS HOUSE
BLOOMFIELD HILLS, MICHIGAN
2003
IKE KLIGERMAN BARKLEY ARCHITECTS

The interior archi-
tecture represents a
melding of influences,
including the English
and Viennese Arts and
Crafts movements and
the Finnish architect
Eliel Saarinen's
Cranbrook Academy
of Art, located a half-
mile from the house.
Quotations from a
range of creators can
be found throughout
the house: Baillie
Scott inspired the
marquetry pattern in
the sitting room, the
dining room ceiling
comes from Sir John
Soane, and Louis Sue
is represented in the
decorative mosaic
panels in one of the
master baths.

Ike Kligerman Barkley Architects has become known for residential projects rendered in sometimes unexpected combinations of historical styles. What elevates the firm's work above pastiche is its in-depth research into the ways in which a particular genre's elements were originally crafted and detailed and how these processes shaped the overall aesthetic.

For this commission, the approach coincided with clients who were attracted to the English Arts and Crafts and Wiener Werkstätte movements, leading them to request a different design treatment for each room. The firm explored multiple historic references using a sumptuous selection of materials, virtually all of which were custom-crafted, hand-worked, or both.

This tactic begins on the exterior, with facades constructed from a specially fabricated diminutive brick ($1^5/_8$ by $6^1/_2$ inches) based on dimensions preferred by the turn-of-the-twentieth-century English architect Sir Edwin Lutyens. Egg-and-dart motifs, abstracted rope profiles, fluting, and scalloping were carved into the limestone chimneys and window bays; cast-bronze leaders and gutters, rendered with multiple levels of embellishment, supply an additional layer of detail.

Within, the house reveals quotations from nearly three centuries of international styles. One of the master baths sets mosaics executed in marble, alabaster, and onyx, in the manner of Art Deco designer Louis Sue, above a carved mahogany vanity and dressing table influenced by Josef Hoffmann. The English Regency master Sir John Soane turns up in the dining room, in the alternation of pattern and color on the ceiling (which is echoed on the floor through a change of direction in the boards). Elements of Lutyens's work at Marsh Court appear in the living room; the marquetry pattern in the sitting room's white oak panels originated with the English Arts and Crafts architect Baillie Scott.

Regarding his firm's appropriations, John Ike has quipped that, given how hard Sue, Soane, Scott, et al. worked to get the details right, he and his partners would be foolish to tinker with them. It would be more accurate to say that this residence represents a judiciously edited compendium of craft-based design, alchemized into originality by the architects' understanding and appreciation of the work's qualities. Pairing this with the clients' commitment to artisanal production has resulted in a house that is both a unified architectural project and a well-curated applied arts collection.

"Different natural materials, all detailed differently, and used in different ways" is how Thomas Kligerman describes the firm's approach to the exterior. The Flemish bond brickwork on the facade is enlivened by a series of angled inserts that meet the rake of the roof; limestone chimneys and window bays were carved with different motifs. The multicolored slate roof thins as it rises from an inch and a half to a quarter inch, a detail drawn from a nearby Bertram Goodhue—designed church.

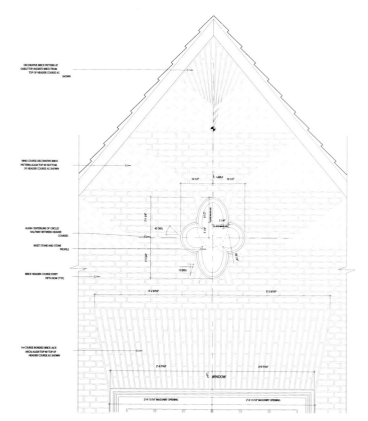

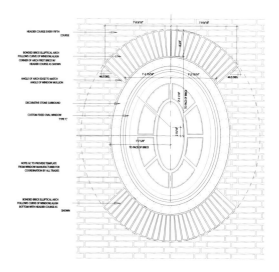

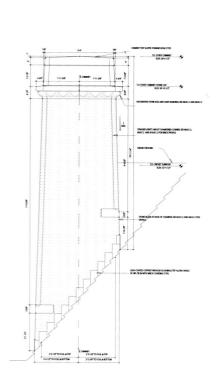

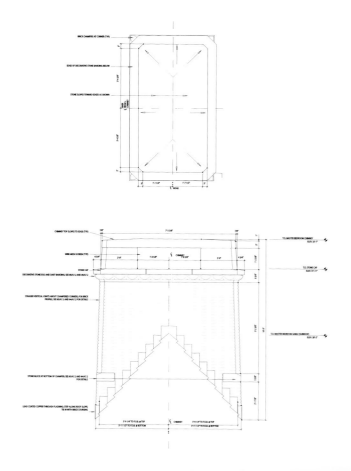

NORWEGIAN NATIONAL OPERA AND BALLET
OSLO, NORWAY
2008
SNØHETTA

When the Oslo- and New York–based firm Snøhetta began work on the Norwegian National Opera and Ballet—a nearly 400,000-square-foot, $320-million complex—the architects were mindful of the fact that, despite the expense, relatively few people would actually use the building. Accordingly, they elevated its public character, conceiving of the theater and forecourt as a single entity, one that ascends from Oslo's fjord and rises to an expansive roofscape, all of it available for climbing, sitting, and sightseeing.

To differentiate between the complex's two programs—the theater and plaza, and the back-of-house operation—Snøhetta enclosed them in two interlocking structures, the former resembling an abstract glacier, the latter rectilinear and boxlike. The difference is heightened by a cladding change: white Italian marble almost entirely covers the "glacier," while the back-of-house is encased in anodized aluminum.

Recognizing that visitors would have an intimate relationship with the building's skin, the architects engaged two teams of artists to articulate the materials. Doing so, they reasoned, would imbue the surfaces with an unusual degree of craft—a tactile effect that might also serve to humanize the monumental structure.

Painter Jorunn Sannes, sculptor Kristian Blystad, and conceptual artist Kalle Grude designed a series of angular ledges that rise from the marble surface, partly to create seating opportunities but also to suggest the uncontainable power of the music within. The trio worked with a factory near Carrara, Italy, to develop a system of machine-hammering a rough texture into the 35,000 marble slabs and used a series of multiscaled Styrofoam models to craft a consistently interesting surface pattern.

To detail the back-of-house aluminum, textile artists Astrid Løvaas and Kirsten Wagle determined that small adjustments could be made to machines producing standardized perforated-metal siding, enabling them to produce made-to-order patterns at a reasonable price. Løvaas and Wagle adapted a textile design found in an antique book and realized it at two scales; the pattern of each 360-by-60-centimeter plate would be a miniature of the one created once they were installed collectively. When test mountings produced unacceptable wind noise, the artists substituted indentations for holes.

The effect is at once contrasting and complimentary. As the hammered stone flows into the indented metal, the mystery of nature dissolves into the Braille-like code of the machine—each the more intriguing for the presence of the other.

To embrace what project architect Tarald Lundevall describes as "the Scandinavian idea of common ownership," the theater's plaza and roofscape were conceived as a single glacier-like object entirely available to the public. The two programs—characterized by Snøhetta principal Craig Dykers as "the opera of the imagination and the back-of-house"—were encased in two interlocking structures. The differences are heightened by a change in cladding: marble for the "glacier," anodized aluminum for the utilitarian component.

Snøhetta turned the articulation of the surfaces over to two different teams of artists. According to painter Jorunn Sannes, who worked on the "glacier," the firm "believes artists look at things in another way, and can go further—extend and strengthen the architects' ideas." On the roof, the textured surface of the layers and ledges of Carrara marble meets the bespoke aluminum facades of the stage tower, which feature indentations and extrusions with the look—and feel— of Braille.

In addition to concealing acoustical material that diminishes the noise level in the lobby, the barklike edges of the oak cladding the tiers imbue the interior with a warmth and texture that mitigate the structure's inherent monumentality. Viewed from the exterior, especially at night, the tiers resemble a massive tree trunk embedded in a vast expanse of ice.

ACKNOWLEDGMENTS

Three angels hover above this book. The first is Andrea Monfried, my editor at The Monacelli Press, who embraced the idea immediately and supportively, gave me a free hand throughout the research and writing processes, and edited the finished text with sensitivity and acuity. The next is Rebecca McNamara, also of Monacelli, who handled the tortuous (and seemingly endless) gathering of images with rather amazing calm and good humor. The third is Claudia Brandenburg, whose book design surprised and delighted me, and ensured that no one will think this is a tome about quilting. Andrea, Rebecca, and Claudia: *thank you.*

My heartfelt thanks as well to the architects, designers, and artisans who permitted me to include their work—and who were generous with their time and observations—and to the photographers whose images interpret that work with insight, immediacy, and elegance.

I discovered a number of the projects included herein while on assignment for different magazines, and I am grateful to the editors who encouraged my interests and offered me a showcase for the results: Kristi Cameron and Martin Pedersen at *Metropolis;* Amber Bravo, Aaron Britt, and Sam Grawe at *Dwell;* and not least my friend Andrew Wagner, first at *Dwell* and then at *American Craft.* Thanks to you all—and for the sustaining years of work as well.

This book owes its variety (actually, its very existence) to the informed and quick-thinking people who helped me to discover its contents: Adam Yarinsky and Stephen Cassell of Architecture Research Office; Laura Briggs and Jonathan Knowles of Briggs Knowles Architecture+Design; Richard Wright of the eponymous auction house; and writer and art adviser Stephanie Murg. I also thank my very good friends Michael Tanner and Dean Kaufman for their flexibility and support—which was above and beyond the call of duty—and Sabrina Orlov and Jennifer Walters for their excellent translations.

My long-suffering wife, Anne, deserves mention for enduring my professional travails and peregrinations with affection and good humor, as do my parents and brother, for decades of uncritical, unambiguous, unstinting belief in me.

Finally, a very special thank you to my agent, friend, and consigliere Jill Cohen, who created an entire career for me and then showed me what to do with it—patiently, selflessly, good-humoredly, and with pitch-perfect judgment. If all writers had Jill in their lives, we'd be the world's happiest professionals.

PHOTOGRAPHY CREDITS

An architecture and design journalist, Marc Kristal is a contributing editor of *Dwell,* a former editor of *AIA/J,* and has written for *Metropolis,* the *New York Times, Architectural Digest, Elle Décor,* and numerous other publications. In 2003, he curated the exhibition "Absence Into Presence: The Art, Architecture, and Design of Remembrance" at Parsons School of Design, and in 2009, he was part of the project team that created the Greenwich South planning study for the Alliance for Downtown New York. Also a screenwriter, Kristal wrote the film *Torn Apart.* He lives in New York.